THE RELATIONSHIP RIDE

ALSO BY JULIA B. COLWELL

*The Relationship Skills Workbook:
A Do-It-Yourself Guide to a Thriving Relationship*

THE RELATIONSHIP RIDE

JULIA B. COLWELL, PH.D.

Copyright 2011
Julia B. Colwell, Ph.D.
www.JuliaColwell.com

Published by Integrity Arts Press

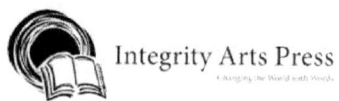 Integrity Arts Press

Integrity Arts Press publishes fiction and non-fiction rooted in the truth that living in integrity fuels joy, supports community, and promotes creativity. In addition to e-books and other electronic means of publishing, we are deeply committed to providing a kinesthetic option for our readers by publishing paper books that can be held, felt, written on, and maybe even hugged. Committed "green," we are ever mindful of our carbon footprint.

Cover Design by Brain Bolts
brainbolts.com

All rights reserved. Printed in the United States of America on recycled paper. No part of this book may be used or reproduced in any manner whatsoever without written permission except in the case of brief quotations embodied in critical articles and reviews.

Library of Congress Control Number: 2 0 1 1 9 2 4 0 9 9

ISBN: 978-0-9830506-2-9

TO KATHRYN,

MY BELOVED

Contents

Dedication   v
Foreword   ix
Acknowledgments   xi
Introduction: Ship of Dreams   xv

I
PREPARING FOR THE VOYAGE

1. Choosing to Leave Safe Harbor   5
2. Getting Your Bearings: The Inner Map   29
3. Getting Your Bearings: The Relationship Map   53
4. Steering to Catch the Wind   67
5. Charting Your Course   95
6. Drain the Bilge!   117
7. Running a Tight Ship   135

II
NAVIGATING THE OPEN SEA

8. Running Aground — Moving Again   161
9. Danger! Storms and Sea Monsters   193
10. Discovering New Worlds   217

Appendix A: Duffle Bag	231
Appendix B: Ship's Locker	247
Notes	255

Foreword

I have had the pleasure of knowing Julie Colwell for many years and have had the double pleasure of watching her fine work blossom and mature. I'm so pleased that she has written this book because her ideas and her warm way of expressing them can now bring joy and fulfillment to a wider audience.

I will let you discover for yourself the pleasures of the metaphors Dr. Colwell uses in the book. Suffice it to say that they make the journey of understanding the ideas very pleasant indeed. Your experience of the book, I predict, will be one of discovering deep wisdom in a gentle, loving way.

Before I invite you to turn the page and begin the ride for yourself, there's one thing I want to make sure you know about Julie Colwell. It's something I want to know about any author in whom I'm going to invest my time and energy. It's this: She practices what she teaches. My wife, Katie, and I have had the pleasure of being with Julie on many occasions, from professional ones such as watching her teach a group, to personal ones such as conversations over a glass of wine at her house. In every situation I've ever seen her in, she is big-hearted, brilliant, and brave—just the qualities I'd want in a companion on any journey.

"Any time not spent on love is wasted," said the philosopher Tasso, so let's not waste any time. Take a big breath, engage your heart and mind, and enjoy the journey.

Gay Hendricks, Ph.D.
Ojai, California
May 2010

Acknowledgments

My heart feels full as I think about the many people whose support gave me the foundation from which to write *The Relationship Ride*. My editor and dear friend, Verna Wilder, guided me gently and determinedly through the whole process, from the first nibbles of ideas through the primitive first attempts to a final product that I feel proud and happy about. Verna showed me how to give my lump of clay its most basic form and then sculpt it with a finer and finer hand so that the result actually looks like what has been in my mind, waiting to be expressed. And she found a way to be simultaneously inspiring, demanding, perfectionistic, and playful so that my process with her has been a surprisingly fun unfolding.

Robbie Staufer (aka Tugboat Robbie) pulled me off of many sandbars. With her whimsical and detailed graphics, she took my concept and developed it into something far beyond what I could have imagined. Eric Boelts' ability to translate what had heretofore existed only in my mind into beautiful cover art warms and inspires me. Between Robbie, Eric, and Verna, I had a crew that I'd sail with anywhere.

Jan Autrey, Kathleen Barney, Cindy Bingham, Jennifer Eads, Robin Galloway, Stacy Gardner, Nancy Kepner, Marianne McCollum, and Kristie Steinbock were instrumental in helping me dive into some new concepts I've been developing and in helping me understand these ideas through their experience and wisdom. The co-creative and inspiring team at Integrity Arts Press—BJ Brown, Kathy Kucsan, Robbie Staufer, Kristie Steinbock, and Verna Wilder—took over the helm to shepherd my manuscript through the details of becoming a real book. In a final stroke of genius, BJ Brown playfully suggested the perfect subtitle.

The Intensive Learning Community at the Boulder Center for Conscious Community (BC3) has similarly been key in the development of new ideas as its members provided a fertile ground for experimentation and feedback. These kindred spirits of the BC3 and I have spent a great deal of time together over the years as we have put our hearts and souls into building community and creating a new way of being in the world, one where love and acceptance combine with the ongoing challenge of evolving to a new level of consciousness.

My clients from the past two decades have been incredible teachers for me. There is no way to describe how meaningful my experience has been through the thousands of hours we have spent together wondering, laughing, raging, crying, and discovering new ways to be. As I've searched for the most effective ways of being a psychotherapist and coach, my clients have given me clear feedback, either directly or simply by what did and didn't help them shift. My course as a psychologist has been totally altered by the winds of what seemed most useful and most true in their lives and my own.

There are many brilliant theorists who have influenced my thinking. David Hawkins' Map of Consciousness gave me new eyes through which to understand what the "truth" is and what it means to evolve as a human. Marc Bekoff's perspective on animals and their emotional and moral worlds allowed me to see how the relationships of the human animal are, in many ways, very much the same as the relationships of our mammalian relatives. The work of Temple Grandin and Peter Levine similarly helped me to draw the connections between animal and human emotional worlds and behavior. Stephen Karpman's classic work on the drama triangle has fundamentally influenced my work. Stephen Porges' polyvagal theory provided the overlap with Hawkins' work, demonstrating how mammals' response to threat mirrors the Map of Consciousness. I am stunned and heartened to understand that the human "ego" is simply our innate animal response to threat.

Gay and Kathlyn Hendricks have been my mentors and teachers for fifteen years. In 1993 when I stumbled upon their groundbreaking book, *Conscious Loving*, I knew that these authors were living masters and that I must study with them. I was right. Gay and Katie's work has literally had an impact on every moment of my life. While I once saw myself and the world through the filter of pathology and dysfunction, I now see possibility and potential everywhere around me. Where many theorists describe the need for evolution of consciousness, Gay and Katie Hendricks have created an elegant, inspiring, and uniquely usable technology for it. They are truly leading us into a new and miraculous world of endless creativity and expansion of consciousness.

Finally, I would like to thank my ultimate teacher, my partner, Kathy. Her kindness, love, passion, and commitment to living from her full creativity inspire me every day. Our twenty-three years together have taken me beyond my wildest dreams as I've experienced nearly every facet of the amazing adventure of deep intimacy. The many challenges that have arisen along the way have allowed me to kitchen-test all of the ideas in this book so that I can personally attest to their effectiveness. And I can especially vouch for the exhilaration of waking up every day to another round on the endlessly fascinating ride of relationship.

Introduction: Ship of Dreams

If you want to build a ship, don't drum up people together to collect wood and don't assign them tasks and work, but rather teach them to long for the endless immensity of the sea.

~ Antoine de Saint-Exupéry

Are you in love with your partner? If so, how do you know? If not, were you ever? When? What was it like? If you can't feel it anymore, what happened? The state of being in love can seem so mysterious. There it is at the beginning, when we don't feel like sleeping or eating and can spend hours just gazing into our new love's eyes. This intense feeling of bliss is one of the best parts of being human. The ecstasy we experience when thinking of or being in the presence of someone we cherish motivates us to make a range of personal sacrifices, to throw caution to the wind, to be willing to behave in impulsive or moony or even goofy ways.

Being in love creates an ongoing sense of intense emotional connection and is a key aspect of sexual attraction and passion. We feel in love with others when we view both them and ourselves as highly valuable at the same time. We are equals in our wholeness; we feel met; we have a sense of touching into the outer possibilities of life through the depth of our connection with ourselves and with the ones we love.

What happens after that initial strike of Cupid's arrow, when we no longer feel those expansive feelings? Our culture seems to share the belief that these intensely blissful feelings will inevitably wane, that riding the amazing waves of this bliss will unavoidably lead to running aground until we finally dismiss the expanded experience of bliss as an illusion. When we buy into this belief, we are ready to accept as truth that the fall from grace into disillusion is a natural progression, and it's unavoidable. We say pragmatically, well, the honeymoon was a fun ride, but now it's over and real life begins. We seem to take the view that a successful long-term relationship is like a ship anchored in a harbor—safe and predictable and inevitably boring. This belief sets up an overall expectation that, in order to experience the tremendous ecstasy of new love, we must wrest ourselves from the familiarity of the "old ball and chain," find a new person, and start over. We often stumble into that process, finding with someone new the awakened feelings we thought we had lost. It is a testament to the intensity of this awakened state that we are willing to go through loss after loss in order to re-experience the wild rapture of bliss once again.

This whole process of finding "in-love-ness" and losing it can seem so mystifying. Because being in love feels so wonderful, we search for explanations as to where those feelings came from and where they went. Here are some popular beliefs:

- The bad shopper: I chose the wrong person. This person is defective, and I'd like to make an exchange.
- "In love" as a virus: It happened to me mysteriously, and it equally mysteriously left. But hey! Now it struck me again—with this new person.
- It's all about romance: If my partner (or I) took time to be more romantic, we could get it back. But for some reason we don't take the time.
- It's not real anyway: I was just infatuated and in the illusion of newness and great sex; nobody is really that wonderful.
- It's time for a new model: Cars get old and so do relationships, so they need to be replaced.
- Long-term relationships require "settling": Being in love is just for those newly together or the young, so we should just re-

sign ourselves to a passionless existence, accepting that we're missing one of life's sweetest gifts. (This one is closely related to the next, and most popular, belief.)
- I love my partner; I'm just not *in love* with him. The death knell of relationships.

What is really going on when we can no longer maintain the most precious part of intimacy with another person? How do we come to give up the ecstasy of sailing with the wind and find ourselves and our relation-ships crashing on the rocks?

An intimate relationship creates the perfect storm of predicament for most of us. It looks like this: We are drawn to the intimacy of connection because we want to be seen, and being seen is like falling in love with our self. We say things like, "I love who I am when I am with her" or "He brings out the best part of me." To truly experience the bliss of intimacy, we believe we must allow ourself to fuse with our partner into the poetic epitome of love: two souls become one. This can feel wonderful, similar to the intense spiritual experience of blending into the cosmos. It is tempting to try to stay in that place of oceanic expansion. But because there are two separate people, we cannot maintain that fused state. The self must pull itself out of the cosmic blend to once again create its own identity.

This transition between intense intimacy and separation is a rocking motion between the need to give up self in order to have connection and the need, after the intensity of merging, to give up connection to regain a sense of self. With awareness, this movement can feel harmonious. However, the merging of selves can bring up fears of engulfment, while traveling out into separateness can trigger past issues of abandonment, turning the smooth rhythm into jarring dissonance.

Self and relationship are impossible to pull apart. Without two equal selves, there cannot actually be relationship; it's just an entanglement.[1] If one person gives up self (which looks like the typical, "I don't care; whatever you want, Honey."), there is no connection, no sense of one person truly meeting the other.

Instead, one person gets to be big while the other is floating around somewhere, diminished by his or her submissiveness.

Similarly, without relationship—that is, without relating to something, anything on the outside of one's inner universe—we cannot have a sense of self. Consider this: Imagine that you are all alone in space.[2] You are bobbing in the great void, nothing for you to interact with. Day after day, you float all alone in the darkness. One day, a fly appears. It buzzes around you. Perhaps you feel annoyed by the buzzing, or happy to have another being to share space with, or curious about what flies are like. Each of these different experiences gives you a sense of who you are, whether you are someone who gets annoyed or likes connection or is curious. Your relationship with the fly is a mirror of who you are.

Without something or someone to relate to, there is no way to learn anything or to know yourself. With a relationship comes endless opportunities to discover, learn, and evolve. If you are willing to notice what is happening inside you, really witness your own experience, you can see who you are right now as well as make choices about who you want to be.

When we make a commitment to another human being, self naturally flows into connection, and within the connection comes a new experience of self: self re-emerges, multidimensional, to create a new type of connection. And so self flows, never the same self, and connection flows, never the same connection. With each movement toward and away from another, we invent a new self, a new connection, like a ship sailing on the ocean, its keel pushing into the sea and the sea pushing into the hull, the ship's prow slicing through wave after wave, never the same combination of boat and sea coming together and moving apart.

Here is the problem: We don't know that relation-ship requires the skills of a seasoned mariner. Lured by the siren call of new love, we tend to jump onboard, fully intending to go on a long journey. When the inevitable challenges occur, however—storms, sandbars, perilous rocks, monstrous waves, and even a variety of sea monsters slithering to the surface—we decide that we made a huge mistake, that we got on the wrong ship, that we didn't really mean to choose this particular crew.

Since most of us don't know what to expect on this wild ride called intimacy, all we can do is hang on. We really do our best in the face of the emotional ups and downs, the intensity of being called to face the unpredictability of the next moment, the emergence of our own or our partner's more challenging aspects. Some people actually thrive with these challenges. Many times, however, we get scared, we withdraw, we shut down. The resulting numbness is what we call "falling out of love." And we find solace in the idea that, really, relationship shouldn't be so hard. And we prepare to abandon ship.

Myth: It Shouldn't Be So Hard

"It shouldn't be this hard!"

I've heard this over and over in sessions with clients.

Whether people are talking about their intimate connections, their families of origin, or their business associates, this plaintive cry comes up again and again. It is as if there is some standard of difficulty that we use to measure whether we are willing to withstand the challenges of relationship, and if we could only apply this standard, we would know if it is worth it to hang in there.

> *Maggie and Pat have been involved for a year. After a very passionate and intense beginning, they now spend much of their time together sniping at each other. An interaction will start out well, but something inevitably sets them off into a bickering battle. Maggie shakes her head sadly when she says with a frown, "My last relationship wasn't ever like this. If it's this hard, it wasn't meant to be!"*

The first time I encountered this idea—that if things were really hard in a relationship, it should end (a sort of euthanasia for an ailing connection)—I was in my late twenties. I was embroiled in ongoing power struggles with my partner of that time, and we finally broke down and called for help. The therapist we saw did her best to help us negotiate through the issues, but after a couple of sessions, she looked at us and uttered those words authoritatively: "It really shouldn't be this hard." Because she was a psychiatrist, I was even more impressed by the terminal diagnosis, and so I quickly put us out of our misery by initiating the breakup.

This idea followed me into my next relationship, so that, with each conflict, I measured it with my own barometer of difficulty. How difficult was this? Too hard? Phew, got through that fight. But—oh no! Here's another one! Maybe two fights in one day added up to "too hard." Or—OK, we're not fighting, but we've had a few days of distance. That's got to mean trouble.

Using this barometer kept me so focused on what was wrong in the relationship that I missed two important aspects: what was working (which, in retrospect, was quite a lot) and what I was learning about life through my partner and our conflicts. My attention stayed on trying to keep the dysfunction from happening, which is about as effective as, say, asking your brain to not think about a pink elephant. I became an expert at noticing and commenting on our problems, which is another way of saying I became very good at criticizing my partner and myself. This orientation meant I could no longer appreciate what was good, including the fertile possibilities for learning that were right in front of me.

Meanwhile I was seeing clients who were either in the middle of relationship trouble or who were coming in because of the painful aftermath of endings. (Couples rarely see a therapist during the thrilling beginnings of intimacy.) I began to appreciate the huge impact connection has on people's moment-to-moment internal worlds and ongoing mental health. There was nothing that triggered more anger, evoked more pain, or created more ecstasy than that energy cord of connection between people. I also noticed a consistent pattern. Conflict and pain would escalate until one of the partners decided that "this is too hard"; someone would press the ejection button to end it all; and there would be a period of relief as both contemplated being out of the relationship. Sometimes, with time to regenerate self and feel the reality of loss, each would reassess and decide to try again.

However, this chipping away at the bond often ultimately resulted in someone making that pronouncement, "See? We just shouldn't be together," finally ending the relationship. Some couples were so shut down by this point that they felt more relief than grief; for most, however, the grief that followed often meant months, perhaps years, of devastating waves of aching loss. I hated that part and wondered what it does to the human heart to sentence it to several rounds of this excruciating process over a lifetime, as a person determinedly continues the search for the perfect relationship, one that wasn't "so hard."

I saw this pattern in friendships and familial relationships and between co-workers as well. People seem to have an ongoing gauge to try to measure when "enough is enough." A friend may seem to need "too much," or the conflict with a parent is unrelenting. Work issues can really take a toll, where it often seems that there are only two options: shut up and take it—or quit. Following those early times when everyone is on their best behavior, issues build until one day the only option seems to be to just get away. Most people I observed did not think to make the key move of turning the blaming finger back around and asking such questions as "What does this have to do with me?" or "What can I learn from this?" or "How am *I* keeping this going?" And so they missed the rich opportunity to shift old unconscious patterns that were keeping them from getting what they really wanted.

Paralleling these observations was my next attempt at intimacy. As I inevitably repeated my patterns and re-created the same old power struggles, I saw only two possibilities:

- It shouldn't be this hard, so I'd better go find someone I'll be

"more compatible" with (which meant going through my own next round of the anguish of loss).
- I was a relationship failure, so I should really be alone.

After a period of despondency accompanied by some desperate introspection ("What am I going to do?! How many more losses am I going to go through before I find the perfect person?? How am I going to be alone? I love being involved with people!!!"), I realized that maybe there is a third option, something like this: Maybe this whole setup is exactly how my higher, bigger, more expanded self put it together for me.

What if the level of difficulty was not a signal that my relationship was in trouble but was instead a beacon from my soul to pay attention? What if relationship—any relationship—was *the* place for our souls to evolve, expand, and grow? What if relationship was a pathway out of the darkness of difficulty—what I thought of as "real life"—and into the more unfamiliar light of joy?

From this perspective, suddenly the idea of "too hard" makes no sense. It is like a scary story we tell ourselves that is so effective we are afraid to leave home because of imagined perils. And in relationship, this particular story gets us to jump ship just as we are making the most headway. There we are, so in the grip of old patterns that we want to flee. We are face-to-face with exactly the issues that are the barriers to our true happiness. With a combination of willingness, courage, and the right skills, that is the moment when we could sweep away our biggest obstacles and find our way back to being in the great flow of life—so long as we don't abandon ship.

Well, I love challenges, so this was a compelling idea. As I pondered this notion, it occurred to me that there really could be no better setup for my own evolution. Let's say I somehow found the exact right person and everything was blissful every day, day in and day out, and we had fabulous sex all the time and I never had a flat tire or was in a bad mood or got lost and I put the exact right amount of money into my retirement account so that all of the financial planners would clap their hands gleefully that I'd accrued the exact right sum when I reached my sixty-fifth birthday.

In fact, many of us hold such a happily-ever-after picture in our heads, which turns out to be impossible to achieve and a setup for frustration, disappointment, and heartache. And, while such an ideal scenario might sound good, there would be nothing to push against, no obstacles to overcome, no way to actually develop beyond where I already was. In the absence of the ongoing challenge that relationship offers, there would be no way for my soul to actually evolve.

Out of Myth and into Reality

The Relationship Ride is not about finding an easy path into a relationship where your every need will be met all the time and you will never have a nasty fight or period of disconnection from your partner, family member, friend, or colleague. This book does not give you a gauge for how long to stay or how to know when to say enough is enough. I now understand how misleading those perspectives can be. They keep our attention on what is wrong with the other or with us, like staring at the bottom of the boat to detect any possible leaks to decide when exactly to abandon ship rather than being present with the glorious feeling of sailing the open sea.

The Relationship Ride offers something much more useful and precious—and fun. It assumes that you and your partner together create the *relation-ship* ride. By coming together, you have set sail into the wide ocean blue, and rather than being at the mercy of the wind or drowning in the waves, you have tools and supplies for a voyage of great adventure: maps (for the inner and external world), a compass (to locate yourself on the maps and set your course), a variety of other necessary instruments, and guidelines for how to steer, how to catch the most wind in your sails, and what to do if a big storm comes through or you run aground.

The voyage of relationship thus allows us to test our mettle with an endless variety of challenges—from rough seas and violent storms to no wind and too much calm. Through our relationships, we become seasoned sailors so that when we come into that final harbor at the end of our lives, we have discovered who we really are, and we have fully lived out our potential.

Choosing this course means steering into the world of possibility, where we can ride the waves and run before the wind, charting a course to the relationship of our dreams.

So which do you choose? Would you prefer to go the unconscious route, pretty much doing what you have always done, letting your automatic reactions lead the way? Most of the world follows this path, and you certainly get to decide if this is the way for you. And I must warn you, once you head into the streaming energy of being conscious, it is not easy to steer back around to the land of the old familiar. What this comes down to now is choosing to remain in the land of the known or to learn to use the tools that will allow you to strike out into the wide-open sea, where your soul will lead the way to your full evolution.

Are You Ready for a Voyage?

Turn the page and take a short quiz to help you decide what to do next.

QUIZ

Are you a landlubber or a sea-bound adventurer?

Scoring: 1: Totally disagree; 2: Disagree; 3: Don't know; 4: Agree; 5: Totally agree

1. I want to live life as an adventure. ____
2. I would like my intimate relationship to be passionate, alive, and long lasting. ____
3. I am willing to look at how I am creating the issues that come up in my close relationships. ____
4. I have old patterns that I would love to shift. ____
5. I am willing to learn a new way to be if it means being happier and freer. ____
6. It's OK with me to be challenged by my relationship. ____
7. I feel ready to face into all of who I really am. ____
8. I'm ready to see what is possible instead of focusing just on what's wrong ____
9. Although there are plenty of issues to deal with, life is full of possibilities. ____
10. I would like to experience as much bliss, in-love-ness, and ecstasy as I can possibly enjoy. ____

TOTAL SCORE: ____

Score Results:

1 – 15:	Stay on land and enjoy the view.
16 – 35:	You might want to read this book and expand your ideas of what is possible.
36 and up:	Come aboard! You're ready to set sail!

I

Preparing for the Voyage

The universe lies before you on the floor, in the air, in the mysterious bodies of your dancers, in your mind. From this voyage no one returns poor or weary.

— AGNES DE MILLE

The notion of sailing off into the wild blue yonder with your beloved sounds romantic, doesn't it? Now think about it in terms of a real voyage: Would you be willing to get on a ship and set sail on the open sea if you had no idea how to steer, set the sails, or chart your way? Yet that is how many of us enter a relationship. Faced with the intricacies of navigation and catching the best wind, not to mention dealing with stormy weather and rocky shoals, how long would it take before you began to squabble? Ran aground, became becalmed, or capsized? Ended up on the rocks? Or decided to jump ship?

Being in an intimate partnership is highly challenging. At best, 50% of couples make it over the long-term. And these are the couples who got through dating and decided to make a commitment. Even knowing these dismal statistics, most of us think we can beat the odds, as if working out the foibles of intimacy is intuitive or a God-given talent. No wonder we hear daily reports of the latest celebrity pair or a friend or acquaintance ending the relationship that they had once extolled as true love. Or we ourselves have to face into one more in a line of painful endings—that is, if we even keep trying to create connection instead of resigning ourselves to the idea that we are just meant to be alone.

Let's change the paradigm. What if you knew that creating deep connection with another human being could be *the* most rewarding accomplishment you could make in your entire life? What if you also understood that intimacy pushes you to the limits of your ability? If you knew that you and your beloved could learn the skills to sail on this daring adventure, would you be willing to spend the time and effort for such an endeavor?

Many of you reading this are already out there in the unpredictability of relationship, finding your way the best you can. Now is the time to drop anchor and rest a bit while you learn a few skills. And for those who aren't currently on the relationship ride and may be wondering if it is worth it to try intimacy again, keep reading! There are real tools that make it possible—and even fun—to navigate through difficulties and sail the big blue expanses of life in relationship.

In the next few chapters you will practice new skills and discover treasures along the way. You might want to dedicate a notebook to recording your responses to the exercises or you can just jot notes to yourself on a pad of paper—whatever works for you. Maps and tools are located throughout the text as well as in the appendices, or you can download them from www.JuliaColwell.com, print them, and keep them available as you read.

So take a few deep breaths and let's get started. Welcome aboard!

I

Choosing to Leave Safe Harbor

We rest here while we can, but we hear the ocean calling in our dreams,
And we know by the morning, the wind will fill our sails to test the seams,
The calm is on the water and part of us would linger by the shore,
For ships are safe in harbor,
but that's not what ships are for.

~ Michael Lille

So many intimate relationships result in disaster: They run aground, sink, capsize, or end up on the rocks. As you begin your preparations for your voyage, it can be instructive to understand what happens that leads to such ruinous endings. Once you have toured this graveyard of lost ships and gained some understanding of how wrecks typically occur, we will spend time examining what creates the conditions where people are thrilled to keep sailing along with each other.

Heading for a Shipwreck

This statistic is commonly known: Half of all marriages end in divorce. For those in gay and lesbian relationships, where statistics on marriage are only beginning to be possible, "serial monogamy"—moving from one committed relationship to another—is often the expected pattern. The beginnings of magical romance and wedded bliss inevitably lead to the realization that sustaining an intimate relationship can be difficult indeed.

What is going on here? From the ongoing litany of love songs, to our fascination with celebrity pairings, to endless TV and romantic movie dramas, our culture pays rapt attention to relationships. And yet we seem to have little idea how to move from the beginning stage of falling in love to creating ongoing, fulfilling, exciting, passionate relationships. What happens that we decide we would rather go through the painful grief of ending a relationship than spend one more second with the person we once declared to be our eternal true love?

Having spent the last two decades counseling hundreds of clients who were wondering where their love went, and meeting the challenge of my own more-than-twenty-year relationship, I have noticed some distinct difficulties that occur time and again for couples. While taking many forms, these problems begin at the same place: people often do not know how to create intimate connection *and* speak the truth about how they feel and what they want. In other words, it is fairly easy to say what we want and how we feel if we don't care about someone else's reaction, and most of us know how to keep our mouths shut about what is really going on in order to preserve the illusion of connection.

But few of us know how to do both—to simultaneously be authentic *and* stay connected. The result is the potential erosion of either our sense of our individual self or our sense of connection with our partner—or both. The combination of giving up our individual feelings and desires and letting go of the precious experience connection brings ultimately gnaws away at the wonderful state of being "in love." Every time we sacrifice who we are for the sake of the relationship ("I don't really care; whatever you want, Honey."), we are throwing dirt on the fires of passion. And every feeling that has not been spoken ("No, I'm fine, really.") creates disconnection and numbing.

The Drop-Off from In Love to "Reality"

The notion of authentic connection has only recently surfaced in our culture, so most of us don't know what that means. And our old models of relationship are not very helpful. The media sound bites of what relationship looks like are generally inaccurate and misleading, typically focusing on the hot and heavy beginnings or on the dramatic and heartbreaking endings. Trying to figure out intimacy through what we observe in the relationships of friends and relatives isn't any more helpful, since generally "dirty laundry" isn't aired in public. Then there are the models of the relationships we are most familiar with—those we observed between our parents, how our parents interacted with us, and whatever went on between our siblings and us. Most of us get our sense of the everyday nature of relationships from family imprinting and the hierarchy and power issues that make up family functioning. Of course there is a huge range of experience in people's upbringings—from loving, kind, and connected to abusive, neglectful, and alienated—leaving each of us with issues from our past that we carry into our adult connections.

Thus our expectations of how to be with our most intimate other—the one with whom daily connection is most vital and to whom our sense of worth is most tied—are a combination of all that we experienced in our families, capped off by the romantic ideals we soak up from the media. This creates the stark drop-off that people often experience from the magical ecstasy of the beginning romance to the frustration and stuckness of the everyday drama of power struggles. The initial connection feels so blissful because we come face-to-face with each other's best, most divine self. However, because people know so little about what produces equal, co-creative relationships, this bliss is almost doomed to erode into power struggle brought about by lapses into hierarchy.

> *Rose and Norman have been together for seven years. Norman recently told Rose that he wants to end the relationship. Rose, shocked and devastated,*

convinced Norman to come in for a session to at least tell her what happened. It became clear during the session that Rose had dominated Norman over the years. Her fears about money were camouflaged by criticism and pushiness. Norman repeatedly gave in to whatever Rose wanted, hoping to please her. This led to Norman's unexpressed, long-simmering anger, which finally erupted into a determined internal push to get himself out of the relationship. By then, he simply had nothing left with which to work on the relationship.

Childhood Patterns Become Power Struggles

People typically do the best they can to move through issues, but without understanding what is really going on under the surface, they can become increasingly frustrated with each other. While the content varies, the cause of the frustration is consistent: Adult relationships drift into patterns that are universal from childhood—that is, parent/child dynamics. One person is in the "power up" (parental) position, while the other takes the "power down" (child) role. These roles can flip within different parts of the relationship—money, household, and childrearing duties, for example—but the stuckness that comes with them is the same.

While these hierarchical roles made sense in childhood, they take adults right into the frustration and quagmire of power struggles.

Tom and Anne were college sweethearts. They've been married fifteen years and have two young children.

Tom works outside the home while Anne stays home with the kids. Tom recently confessed to Anne that he'd been having an affair with a colleague from work for the past six months. In our sessions, Tom speaks authoritatively while Anne listens. Her words are less assured, though she has been having rages at home.

These begin with angry verbal outbursts at Tom's betrayal and end with several days of her barely speaking to him. He has been tolerating this because of his guilt about the affair, though his impatience with her process is showing. As the dynamics between them unwind, it becomes clear that Tom feels powerful at work but has difficulty entering into the world of Anne and the kids when he comes home. He tries to seize control by playing raucous games with the kids, which annoys Anne because he is disrupting what she sees as a placid family scene. The affair allowed Tom to once again feel significant and valued, having lost his place of importance with Anne as she focused more on the children.

Power struggles create a knot that can tighten and tighten until it becomes increasingly difficult to untie. The inevitable conflicts of needs and desires that occur for a couple can activate unconscious patterns from past stressful experiences. This is when communication really has the potential to deteriorate. As each person reacts, stress levels increase. The brain's response to stress is to shut down the least necessary systems (like analysis and complex problem-solving) so that the threat can be dealt with through its more basic systems—to fight, to strike, to flee, to become immobilized. Thus, the perceived threat triggers people out of their creative and cooperative selves into increasing contraction and reactivity.

Threat Response Leads to Escalation

Contraction plus reactivity, while helpful for animals that must quickly take action, is a bad combination for communication between humans. Instead, these two states lead to a cycle of defense and counter-defense. If we don't have the skills to shift out of this cycle, we react to the escalation from our primitive brains. With each succeeding round of this pattern, we begin to feel and sound more and more like animals fighting for survival. Strategies of "reflective listening" (or other cognitive approaches still taught by many couples' therapists and attempted by earnest couples), are rendered impossible. This inability to de-escalate can lead to a disheartening sense of failure and the belief that there is something terribly wrong with the partnership—all because the primitive brain is doing its job of defending against threat.

Let's take this one step further so it is really clear. When we feel good, we are calm, relaxed, soothed, and alert. Intimate connection enhances those sensations as we cuddle up with each other, look deeply into each other's eyes, and let ourselves rest in the warmth of intimacy. Under those circumstances, our communication is fine. We know how to talk with each other when we are in this calm, relaxed state. We don't need any workshops or facilitators to help us speak and listen to each other. We can solve problems, hear what our partner is saying, admire and appreciate all the beauty of ourselves and each other, and know that our partner is our ally. Then something happens to trigger us, something that tells our automatic threat system we are in danger. This is when communication deteriorates.

John Gottman,[3] who has conducted twenty-five years of in-depth research on couples and their physiology during conflict, illustrated the effects of varying arousal levels with a brilliant piece of research. While videotaping arguing couples, the research associates waited until the conflict had escalated and then suddenly stopped them, telling them the camera had broken. The couple was directed to sit silently until the camera was repaired (which was easy to do, since it was not actually broken). After fifteen minutes, the associate told the couple that the camera was fixed, so they could continue the argument. What they found surprised them: The couple was physiologically and cognitively completely different. Each person had calmed down, so now they were able to easily work out the issue. Gottman postulated that the fifteen-minute interval was enough for each person to move out of the fight-or-flight response so that adrenaline was metabolized, blood pressures dropped to normal, and pulses slowed. Once out of their highly aroused state, couples could typically communicate just fine.

The threat response creates other problems in intimacy. When our brains are triggered and we move out of relaxed alertness into heightened awareness, one of the first shifts we make is to figure out "what's wrong." Our brains are supposed to do this. We have to know if that's a mountain lion behind the tree or if the rock is going to fall on our head, so we need to be able to notice the problem and react to it. But in relationships, this means we automatically pay attention to what our partner is doing that we don't like (also known as becoming critical). And of course, the natural response to being criticized is to contract and defend oneself. This is how the reactivity/contraction cycle can really pick up momentum. From relaxed, calm, and alert, we move into the classic fight-or-flight state, preparing to fight our way out or run away, both responses that tend to heighten the situation. If the escalation continues to intensify, our brains—perceiving the highest level of threat—might move us to the ultimate response, which is either to become immobilized (an animal's attempt to shut down all circuitry before being killed) or to launch an all-out attack (the snake's strike). We go from our most connected selves to a mammalian response of fighting or fleeing to a reptilian response of freezing or striking.

Threatened Humans Resemble Threatened Animals

Listen to the language we use to describe these sorts of human interactions; you can hear these lurking animal survival selves: "Don't bite my head off" or "You are attacking me!" or "He's going for the jugular." Barking, bull-headed, back-biting, snarling, snapping predators go after the weak, who run away when they can or roll over, submit, collapse, and freeze when they can't. We know to fear the reptilian folks even more. These are the ones who are cold, unfeeling, cruel, poisonous, venomous, chilling, cold-hearted, and downright mean.

What is the significance of these lists? It is hard to face, but we all have all of these qualities somewhere within us. It is how we evolved. As much as we may want to believe that these words describe other people and not us, under the right circumstances every one of us is capable of behaving like a threatened mammal or reptile. Our larger culture's judgment of these qualities as beastly, despicable, horrible, and the like conditions us to disown these parts of ourselves, push them so far out of our consciousness that we cannot access them—except, of course, with our most intimate other. With all of this in mind, let's take a look at the progression from romantic bliss to "I don't love you anymore—I'm leaving."

The Progression from "In Love" to "I'm Leaving"

Two people meet and show each other their best selves, the parts that are sweet and caring and loving. They feel wonderfully expansive, close to bliss. The romance of the beginning of relationships, the celebrated "honeymoon" period, is about feeling great about oneself and one's partner. During this time people behave at their very best and walk around seeing themselves and their new partner as quite wondrous and their lives as endless in possibility and potential. They give up sleep and food for the ecstasy of sex and connection. The soothing and cuddling that is emblematic of this beginning time allow the brain to access its most creative functioning. It is from this place that people create poetry, art, and music, extolling the virtues of their love. In fact, the true sense of being "in love" is about feeling wonderful about who we are when we are around our partner because the circumstances of this time allow us to contact our most highly creative, loving, and most evolved selves.

However, the merging of selves that occurs during the honeymoon phase cannot last. This beginning sense of oneness must ultimately shift into each person regaining his or her full self. In fact, relationship is ultimately the pulsation of moving from deep connection to individuality, back into connection, and so on. To master this rhythm is to create a thriving relationship, one that allows for both intense intimacy and a strong expression of individuality. However, each swing from one pole to the other holds its own challenge. Letting oneself fall into the amorphousness of intimacy can bring up old fears of losing oneself that most of us seem to carry. Fully experiencing one's separateness, one's individuality, can rattle awake the existential terror of aloneness.

In the middle of this difficult emotional challenge to create connection and self, real life jumps in: something happens. (In this material world, something will always happen to challenge our calm state, generally several times a day.) Compared with the ecstasy and harmony at the beginning of relationship, the "something" that happens can feel disappointing, or we might see it as an indication that something is really wrong instead of simply recognizing the natural progression of any relationship.

Few people have the skills to handle the emotional turmoil that can erupt when *something happens*. Riding the waves of intense feelings and old issues brought up by intimacy and individuality—as well as our reactions to the "somethings" that happen—challenges the most experienced emotional surfers. Often the best we can do is to resort to the familiar old coping strategies we brought into the relationship. We start by being reasonable, trying hard to be good partners. If that does not work—because we are tired or stressed or we've triggered some old pattern—the next step is to revert to childhood strategies. These can range from withdrawing and shutting down emotionally, to placating and pleasing, to having temper tantrums (be they mild whining or explosive rages), to manipulating and using passive-aggressive behaviors (like being late or forgetting agreements).

> *Matt and David had a whirlwind romance. They moved in together and felt blissfully happy as they created the home each had always wanted. After the first year or so, however, they found themselves disagreeing more about little things, like who should go grocery shopping and how to clean the bathroom. Matt started being more critical of David, who responded by trying harder to please Matt. But he also began to stay at work a little later. Matt would call to find out when David was going to come home; David would give him a time and roll in thirty minutes or an hour late, leading to a heightened round of criticism from Matt.*

As life continues its steady pulsation of tossing stressful events into the partnership, the initial agreeableness can begin to wear down. At some point, our willingness to just "let it go" corrodes, and we feel pulled to stand up for ourselves. Our animal selves show up, which is why the strategy of compromising has a limited shelf life; sooner or later, the part of us designed for survival just will not give up on what it really wants. Power struggles escalate. Without skills to shift out of the threatened brain, each person is prone to behaving in an increasingly animalistic manner, striking out, attacking, wounding, hurting. Or we collapse, freeze, roll over. All of these experiences leak out some inner "bad" self that most of us do not want to expose, yet here it is, leaping to the surface like a jack-in-the-box that cannot be shoved back into its container.

From Lover to Fighter

Our animal energy, however, is not only destructive. It also contains the wildness that fuels our passion and drive. It is the energy of our creativity. However, combining this animal energy with human cognition can create problems—namely, the drive to want to be right and the urge to fight "to the death" to not lose conflicts. Power struggles are fueled, risking this becoming an entrenched pattern of the relationship. Depending on how much the couple gets mired in these struggles, it can be easy for each person to drift from the thoughtfulness, consideration, kindness, and empathy that are the hallmarks of two people at the beginning of the relationship. Once activated, the threat brain turns the partner into enemy, not ally, and suddenly our goal is to defend ourselves. The fight mode itself brings forward such useful but unsavory characteristics as scoring points by finding the other's weakness, being selfishness, being critical, counterattacking, emotionally withdrawing, being cold, or collapsing. The need to be a fighter, not a lover, has taken over.

Because we do not want to see these characteristics in ourselves, we try desperately to shut down our emotional world, leading to disconnection from our self and from our partner. This emotional shutdown takes a lot of energy because we have to fight to keep feelings out of our conscious awareness. Addictions like drinking, smoking, shopping, working, and watching TV can help us control our emotions. Unfortunately, all of these approaches mean we are withholding important information from ourselves and from our partners, which leads to the same consequence: distance and disconnection.

> Peter and Amy had been married for five years when Amy became attracted to someone from work. Her marriage to Peter seemed fine, so she wasn't sure how she got drawn into this affair. As we looked under the surface, however, it was clear that Amy and Peter had slid into unconsciousness with each other. After several fights that went nowhere, they simply distanced from each other so that they didn't have to experience the frustration of unresolved conflict. Amy became increasingly lonely in the marriage but didn't know what to do to regain the original closeness she had felt with Peter. She didn't want to end the marriage because it gave her some sense of security. Her affair allowed her to stay in the marriage and to connect with someone who seemed to value who she really was. It seemed like a good solution—except for the lying.

An associated problematic outcome is that being around people other than our partner does not usually bring up these most primitive emotions, which elicits this logical conclusion: "I only feel this bad around you. Therefore, you are causing me to feel this way. I want to be with someone I can feel good about myself with."

> After two years together, Maggie and Pat were fighting all the time. Maggie believed she'd feel better if Pat would be soft and attentive with her, so she criticized her every time Pat was her typical sarcastic self. Pat argued that she could be softer if Maggie would stop being so critical. These arguments escalated, and each was willing to be more hurtful in her own defense.

They finally ended their relationship: each woman said she just couldn't stand how the other viewed her.

Evolving from Hierarchy to Equality

Hierarchy—another dynamic that humans inherited from the animal kingdom—creates an additional layer of difficulty in creating connection. The idea of the dominant one that rules the pack or herd to create increased safety and protection is familiar to us. We have adopted the social hierarchy of many animal species into our military and businesses with the typical structure of a chain of command. Fundamentalist religions teach the necessity of male domination over females and children in an attempt to create structure and clarity and to teach their children the values they believe will keep their pack safe.

Hierarchy may have had a place in human relationships through the centuries by increasing our survival rates during war, famine, hardship, and the countless challenges we have faced over time. However, in the past decades as our consciousness has substantially evolved, our ability to live beyond simple survival has shifted. We now prize equality of race, gender, nationality, and sexual orientation as we never have before. Suddenly we are faced with a new pressure on—and possibility for—intimate relationships: how to live as equals.

There is a big problem with this new possibility: Few people know how to live intimately in this paradigm. We don't have much experience of it in our closest relationships. We know how to be "Power Under": we have all been children raised by adults. We know how to follow rules, comply, do as we are told, even if we are secretly (or openly) rebelling. And we know how to be "Power Over": we might have to learn to be parents, teachers, and bosses, but we have plenty of role models. We've observed how to control others, demand, direct, teach, manage. Whether or not we actually step into these roles, they are familiar to us.

Notice the structure of relationships. Like a Russian nesting doll, there are several layers. On the outside is our social self, generally able to access the most complex brain functions. We can connect with others and play well, knowing how to value people around us and feel relaxed and soothed in connection.

When all is well, we maintain eye contact, we feel creative, we are willing to play and experiment with new experiences: we feel the most expanded, most like our true selves. This is what most of us mean by being happy: that we are moving through the world with ease and feeling good about how we are showing up.

But then, of course, *something happens*. If we are not consciously present to slow down or divert our body's automatic reactions, our threat brain—or Reactive Brain—will turn on. Now we are back in our primitive animal self with the deeply ingrained tendency to revert to dominance/submission, the hierarchy of the pack. The fragile connection to being equal partners—that is, "Power With"—is no longer available to us. We move out of equality and connection and resort to the part of the brain that has aided animal survival for millions of years. This shift to fight/flight/freeze/strike, which leads to a hierarchical dominance/submission structure, leaves us in the clutches of power struggle. Our previously much-loved partner is now the enemy, and our ally becomes our foe. The brain is doing exactly what it was designed to do when it quickly focuses on its immediate survival: react to danger.

> *Patricia and Bonnie had a pattern of creating arguments first thing in the morning. The root cause was unclear; there was tension at the breakfast table as they went through the frenzy of preparing for the day, getting out the door. One morning, Patricia came downstairs and found the dishes Bonnie hadn't done the night before. When Bonnie came into the kitchen, Patricia pointed at the full sink in exasperation. Bonnie rolled her eyes, which got Patricia started on the other complaints she'd stored up: when would Bonnie ever do what she said she'd do, how hard could it be, and what about those bills that hadn't been paid yet? Bonnie fired back about how Patricia was so critical and how she was tired of never having fun anymore. After a couple of rounds of this, Bonnie picked up a bagel and threw it at Patricia. Patricia, her face*

showing disbelief and fury, stomped out of the kitchen. Bonnie lay her head down on the table and sobbed.

The bottom line of being in a reactive survival mode is that we feel *terrible*. We do not want to behave like threatened animals; we generally want to be kind and loving and good. So we try to figure out what made us go to this awful place. And what do we see most clearly as the cause? Our partner. We felt fine before her voice had that tone or he was late or he said the thing we told him not to say because it sounds just like our father. It is so logical. And our clear task, then, is to teach the partner how to do whatever helps us feel good and stop doing whatever makes us feel bad.

The Tyranny of "The List"

At one point in my relationship with Kathy, I had my list and she had hers. I had told her—many times!—if she would just smile at me when I walked in the door, I would feel welcomed. I had also instructed her to try to be more thoughtful, not talk to me much in the morning, and couldn't she just be a little more romantic? And by the way, a few cards or words of appreciation would be nice.

Then she had her list. Let's see—pay more attention to the dogs, don't be late—or at least call her if I was—clean up my piles of stuff—oh, and something about—what was that? Was I supposed to give her space when she was mad or give her a hug? Hmmm. It's kind of blurry...

The problem with this approach is that, try as we might, no one can remember everything on the other's list. (In fact, when we are in Reactive Brain, it is hard to remember our *own* lists.) And if there is a conflict, for sure we are going to stop trying to please the other. So now there are more reasons to feel bad about ourselves and about our partner. If we—or they—really cared, we—or they—would try harder. Isn't that what relationships are about?

One of Maggie's main complaints about Pat was that Pat just didn't care about her. If she did care, she would try harder to really be there for Maggie, especially when Maggie was tired or emotionally over-wrought. But she didn't want Pat to cramp her style when she wanted space. Pat had tried hard to comfort and soothe Maggie but then got confused and angry when Maggie told her she'd read the signals wrong, that she wasn't tuned in enough to see this was not the right time.

From Cooperation to Win/Lose

It is a predictable progression. Two people can be feeling connected and loving with each other and in the flow of cooperation and sense of unlimited possibilities. Once one is triggered, however, the feelings of connection disappear in a flash. In its place is the world of the threatened animal: scarcity, competition, survival of the fittest. The range of solutions that had been available before the conflict now narrow to one goal: winning. "It's my way or the highway." Now it is each person for herself, fighting to get her needs met. This is a vitally important moment in relationships. Where both had been open to what was mutually beneficial, now they are focused on win or lose. While winning feels good, the real goal here is not to lose because this means being a loser, being the one who is humiliated, defeated. For many, this becomes a fight for survival of self. What was a simple issue is now about saving face, holding on to one's sense of being all right.

At this point fights escalate. This happens for individuals, it happens for groups, it happens for countries. For humans, getting activated into threat mode means that our pride is at stake. While animals might snarl at each other or ram horns for a while until each backs away, people have the blessing—and curse—of trying to make meaning out of conflict. The combination of animal threat brain and human consciousness can be a volatile mix: When we are triggered, we are willing to sacrifice our reason, our reputations, and our relationships to keep our pride.

When this brain activation occurs, people move out of their expanded, biggest selves and start to regress through the stages of evolution. We begin with a commitment to being allies who co-create amazing possibilities. Then the trigger occurs—something happens—and the couple's vision collapses into "either/or" (either you get what you want, or I get what I want; we can't both get what we want). If the conflict escalates further, it can become a fight to win at all costs. The ultimate escalation? The reptilian willingness to strike with venom, to go for the kill. This devolution of humans to cold-blooded monsters is evident, for example, in the consequences of domestic violence.

Automatic Physiological Reactions

While couples might see their own proclivity to become activated into their bestial selves, they typically have no idea what to do about it. One response is to resort to automatic strategies, those they devised as children in reminiscent circumstances and that actually resemble the functioning of animals under threat. Notice what these look and feel like:

- *Fight*, of course, is easy to see: people get angry, raising their voices and curling their fists, as their blood pressure, pulse, and stress hormones shoot up.
- *Flight* can be as obvious as someone simply leaving (or threatening to leave) but can also be subtler, turning into an unwillingness or even inability to keep talking and avoidance of intimate contact.
- *Freeze* is the ultimate brain response to threat and includes shutting down much of the nervous system (the animal's physiological preparation to avoid feeling the pain of injury and death[4]). As such, it can be more difficult to observe from the outside and is one of the most difficult responses to reverse from the inside. The human version of freezing can include feeling paralyzed, which can appear to be stonewalling; or dis-

sociating, an overall emotional shutdown and disconnection from one's internal and external worlds.
- *Strike* is the unpredictable, seemingly uncontrollable response from deep in the brain, where, once unfrozen, aggression is deadly as a snake's poison bite.

Without understanding how the body's most basic systems tend to take over automatically, couples incorporate these responses into what they fight about. Complaints like, "Why won't you talk to me!" or "I can't believe you're so angry over something this stupid" or "You can't leave! We're not done talking!" demonstrate people's belief that their partners should be able to override their physiology. This can lead to the game of hot potato pathology—who is there something wrong with? Is it me? No, it's you! No, you! OK, it's me.

From his extensive research on what causes marriages to fail, John Gottman has identified what he calls "the Four Horsemen of the Apocalypse."[5] When he and his team go over videos of couples fighting, if they find these four indicators, they can predict with 90% accuracy which couples will be divorcing in the next four years. The Four Horsemen are Criticism, Defensiveness, Stonewalling, and the ultimate—Contempt. Notice how each of these can be paired with fight/flight/freeze/strike—that is, we attack (fight) through criticism and defensiveness; flee and freeze by stonewalling; strike through contempt. Without understanding their own physiology, couples create communication habits that will, with great probability, finally sink their relation-ship.

Most other classic relationship problems result when people try desperately to deal with their unpredictable and confusing physiology. Remember that when they start out, almost all couples want their relationship to succeed. But watch the progression:

1. All is well; there is a sense of connection and relaxation.
2. Something happens. One or both perceive a threat.
3. The fight/flight/freeze/strike response gets going. Without

tuning in to this, people force themselves to "communicate" through it.
4. Escalation occurs. Someone yells; someone leaves; someone shuts down; someone gets mean. The nervous system of each person is aggravated and agitated.
5. Substances help settle us down, so we resort to addictions—drugs, alcohol, cigarettes, sugar, computer games, TV, Internet—to soothe and comfort ourselves.

And it continues. Distance from the partner feels somewhat better, allowing each to come back to baseline in his or her physiology. Maybe one or both get outside support. Now they have the opportunity to describe the scary experience. Since few of us have the skills to look at our own behavior squarely, describing the experience means telling a friend how terribly our partner treated us. Suddenly a whole story is developing about how bad the other person is, leading to questions from friends and family like, "Why are you still with this person?" or this provocative and seductive opening for an affair: "You don't deserve to be treated like that. I respect you. I cherish you." If we do not find a better way through this maze, the bliss we felt about ourselves and our beloved at the beginning turns into the horror of seeing a mirror of our worst selves. That can translate into feeling at our worst when we are with our partners. But that new person makes us feel so good . . .

So many of the problems that humans experience begin in the middle of this swirl of trying hard to be good people while being overtaken by our animal physiology and response to threat. Poor communication. Power struggles over sex, money, housework, the kids, and the in-laws. Lack of intimate connection. Anxiety, depression (both signals that we are not skilled at managing the nervous system's responses). Addictions of every variety (also our attempts to soothe ourselves, as well as to create some sense of aliveness in the middle of stressful circumstances). Affairs. And ultimately, if there is no alternate route found through the difficulties, chronic illness.

Making It Through to Smooth Sailing

All right, Sailor, have you learned enough about what can go wrong? Ready to turn your attention to what can happen if you know how to traverse these difficulties? Would you like a preview of how to map a passage through the rocky shoals and stormy seas so you can experience the bliss of smooth sailing?

Because few people understand what is really going on beneath the surface of intimate interactions, the typical experience of moving through dangerous waters is to hold one's breath and hope for the best. Sometimes this works; often it leads to a great deal of frustration. The antidote is to be conscious: to become aware of our unconscious, automatic patterns and shift them. It is the difference between trying to move a fog-bound ship and steering by the North Star.

Becoming conscious can change the trajectory of conflict when we become aware of critical choice points. Using the powerful tools you will be learning, let's walk through the process of escalation described above to see where we can make conscious choices that de-escalate conflict.

1. All is well; people feel connected and blissful.
2. *Something happens.* One or both perceive a threat.
3. The fight/flight/freeze/strike response gets going.
4. One of two things can happen at this point:
    - One or both people notice this and take action—breathing, moving, describing their physical sensations. Adrenaline has time to be metabolized; nervous systems have time to settle. (Skip to step 6.)
    - OR they miss the opportunity to be conscious, and escalation occurs. The yelling, leaving, shutting down, getting mean happens, leading to agitated nervous systems. (Proceed to step 5.)
5. One or both stop and tune in to realize that they are reacting

with their primitive brains. They take time to tune in to their bodies and describe whatever is happening physically.
6. They take effective action to soothe themselves by deep breathing, meditating, taking a hot bath, going for a walk, wrapping in a blanket, drinking tea. Without trying to process further, they simply take the other person's hand, offer body contact.

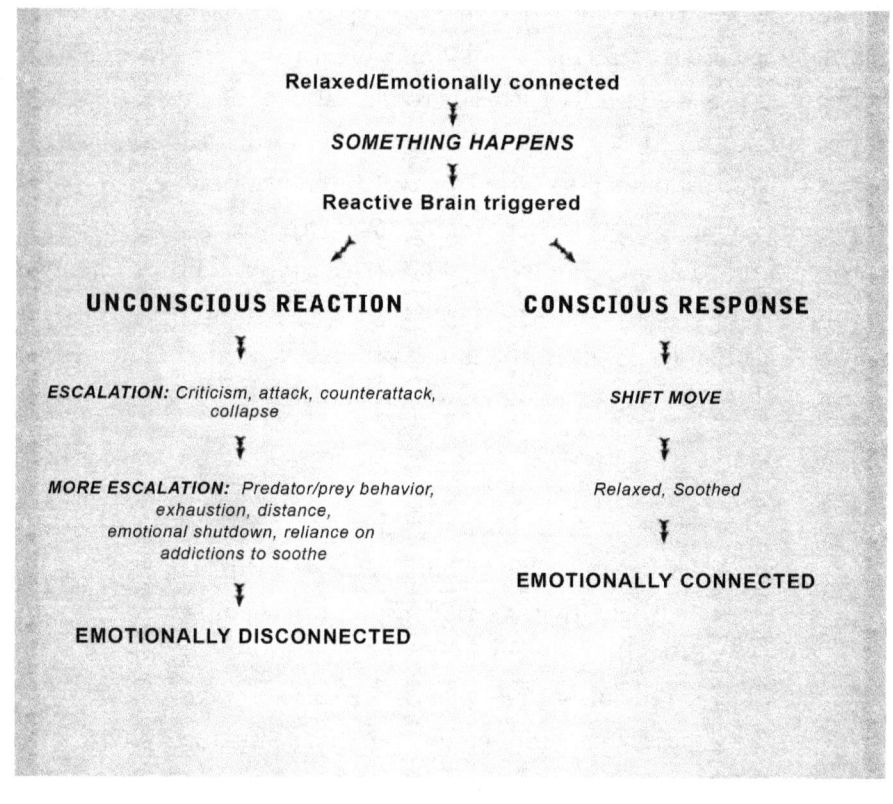

What if they missed that moment at step 4 and just keep struggling? There are still many opportunities to become conscious—with each breath, really. They can watch their negative thoughts, challenge themselves to appreciate, wonder, "How am I keeping this going?" When they call friends for support, if they are lucky they can access a community of folks who will challenge each to look at the unconscious pattern that is being acted out instead of acting as a "glue club," a term Gay Hendricks coined to refer to people who help keep couples stuck by supporting the view that the partner is wrong.

Each of these moves can lead to the nervous system ratcheting down out of arousal and activation. As the nervous system comes back to baseline, thinking can clear. Now the Reactive Brain can shift out of the automatic view of partner-as-enemy. As the fog clears, each person can once again remember the best parts of the other and start to recall why closeness felt safe.

Notice how much potential the conscious path has for growth. Intimate relationship has the inimitable ability to trigger one's deepest patterns and unearth them from the most submerged parts of self. Such excavation can make us feel pretty unstable about who we are, but it can ultimately lead to trading in old, automatic patterns for new ways of being. If people had confidence in their ability to survive this mining of their personality, they might even seek out the most challenging relationships in order to maximize this possibility for transformation.

While the beginning bliss of relationship can feel fantastic, the strong pull to be on one's best behavior can be exhausting. At the start of relationships, we are motivated to be charming, sweet, generous, selfless—in short, to show our best selves. This is clearest when new loves talk about past relationships, and it is so easy to see how the ex-partners were the reason for the demise of those connections. But as the "somethings" happen, and each person's Reactive Brain gets activated, the rest of the story begins to emerge. About a year into a relationship, the new love might want to meet up with the ex to commiserate about the unpleasant aspects of being with this partner.

Seeing the "negatives" about each other could give partners a reason to end the relationship and look for a less defective model. But here is the sweet possibility: to be loved for one's whole self. All of it. All of the best parts, all of the worst parts. The kindness, courage, compassion, intelligence; the meanness, cowardice, insensitivity, stupidity. We all have all of it. When our more dense and contracted aspects—those parts of us that get expressed when we are frightened, angry, sad, or otherwise feeling threatened— come into the open, we can begin to interact with them in a way that can really heal them. Brain research is clear: there is nothing like the soothing comfort of intimacy to allow those most wounded parts of us to be transformed.

Intimacy: The Perfect Crucible for Transformation

In fact, if one were to devise a method for human evolution, it would be difficult to come up with anything better than close relationship. Intimacy creates the perfect crucible for human transformation. Energy rises within connection; the intensity of love allows for space within which old, dense patterns can arise and be cleared out. If people do not expect this energetic purification, it can be very unpleasant, and indeed, seem like a reason to abandon ship. But if we are conscious and prepared, being in a relationship can give us a ride beyond our wildest dreams.

Exercise: Taking Your Pulse

- Learn how to take your pulse. (One easy way is to press two fingers against the jugular vein in your neck for a minute, counting the beats.)
- For the next week, notice when you are frightened or angry, and take your pulse. Notice whether it is more than ninety beats per minute, the point at which John Gottman[6] says we should stop trying to process an issue.
- After fifteen minutes, take your pulse again. If it has dropped to below ninety beats per minute, notice if your thinking has changed since the first check.

Points to Steer By

- Few of us know how to simultaneously be authentic and stay connected.
- Adult relationships drift into patterns that are universal from childhood—that is, parent/child dynamics.
- Perceived threat triggers people out of their creative and cooperative self into increasing contraction and reactivity.
- Every one of us is capable of behaving like a threatened mammal or reptile.
- To master the rhythm from a sense of oneness to separateness and back again is to create a thriving relationship. However, each swing from one pole to the other holds its own challenge.
- The strategy of compromising has a limited shelf life; sooner or later, the part of us designed for survival just will not give up on what it really wants.
- We are now faced with a new pressure on—and possibility for—intimate relationships: how to live as equals.
- Intimate relationship has the inimitable ability to trigger one's deepest patterns and unearth them from the most submerged parts of self. This can ultimately lead to trading in old, automatic patterns for new ways of being.
- There is nothing like the soothing comfort of intimacy to allow those most wounded parts of us to be transformed.
- Intimacy creates the perfect crucible for human transformation.

2

Getting Your Bearings: The Inner Map

I must go down to the sea again, to the lonely sea and the sky;
And all I ask is a tall ship and a star to steer her by.

~ John Masefield

It is easy to imagine the skills you need to sail a ship: You want to get good at navigation, which includes pinpointing your current location, charting a course to your destination, and choosing the most efficient way to get there. And of course you need to know how to steer through storms and what to do if you run aground or are blown off course. It is helpful to be able to pump out the bilge, to plug leaks, and to know how to catch the best wind. And on those really long voyages, it is useful to know how to handle the slimy monsters that inevitably will emerge from the deep and threaten to pull your relation-ship under.

Before we get to these more advanced skills, let's get our bearings by becoming familiar with the workings of the inner world.

The Art of Navigation

The art of navigation requires moving back and forth between locating yourself on a map and using your compass to set your course. In this chapter you will learn how to get your bearings so you know where you are, no matter what storms are swirling inside or outside of you.

It is easy to get lost in the upheavals of emotional connection and expression that come with being in a relationship. One moment you're feeling like all is well, and then—zap!— something happens to toss you off center. You open a bill or slip on the ice or read your partner's upset expression or hear the latest dire report on global warming. Suddenly your sense of well-being has changed to something else. Noticing what is going on with you in the middle of the upheaval is the first step to being able to shift back to well-being. It's like finding yourself on a mall directory: *YOU ARE HERE*. Then you can map the route to where you want to go.

Your Inner World: What Your Body Knows

You are living in a skin that is wrapped around a fascinating universe. Take a moment to notice the extensive range of processes going on inside of you right this instant: thoughts rising and falling away; sensations tell you whether you are hungry or over-stimulated or sleepy; systems like breathing, blood flow, and heart rate taking care of themselves. In addition to all of that inner activity, the outside world might be drawing your attention to what you see, hear, and smell, as well as what you taste and touch.

Many of us have learned to shut off the experience of noticing what is going on in our inner world. Maybe we have been taught to tune only into our thinking minds and value ideas over body sensations. With this focus, we may have little idea how to notice the feelings coming from the rest of our inner world, even those sensations that are loudly trying to get our attention. The pain of a headache, the cramp in a lower back, the tightening of a stomach are all signals that we might have learned to turn off with a variety of medications or substances, believing that what matters most is what our minds tell us.

Retraining ourselves to notice our bodies' messages is key to navigating through life. To get your bearings, your internal perception of anything going on in your body is your primary way to locate yourself. Imagine that your body is a finely tuned communication device that is constantly sending you messages about your experiences. While your mind spins all kinds of believable—yet untrustworthy—stories about reality ("No one understands me." "My partner is inconsiderate." "Life is hard."), your body gives you accurate feedback about how you are interacting with the world. It is quite miraculous, really: your physical sensations are often signals linking you to your emotional responses. In other words, there is a brilliant stream of feedback between whatever is occurring in the outside world and your own individual, unique experience of those events in your inside world. In fact, what is going on in your body is really how you know you are different from anyone else. When you tune in to it, your headache could be a sign that you are tired, dehydrated, or angry; your cramping back, that you need to move around or express your irritation; your tight stomach, that you are actually scared, not mad. It is very simple, really: your physical sensations are *the* connection to your emotional self. And you are the only one who gets to decide what is really true about your own experience.

In a moment you will close your eyes and check in to see what is going on inside your body. You will take a long breath in and wander around in there, looking for any physical sensation that is trying to get your attention. It might be tightness or clenching, or it may be a sense of flow and expansion. It might be a very loud sensation ("MY NECK HURTS!") or something quite subtle ("There's a slight tingling down the back of my left hand").

Exercise 1: Checking In with Your Body

- Close your eyes and take an inventory of everything you can notice that is happening inside of you.

- Identify at least five different sensations before you open your eyes again.
- What was happening in there?

Our bodies were designed to feel good, to have sensations of expansion, openness, and flow. We try to do things to make those feelings happen because they are so satisfying and enjoyable. The more we tune in to these wonderful sensations, the more we get to fully enjoy them. Being in love is one of the most expanded experiences that many of us have, and one that we will go to great lengths to create. Other routes to less intense but still positive feelings include exercising, laughing, being in nature, meditating, playing—it's a long list. When we don't feel expanded, we may call ourselves "depressed" and use a variety of prescriptions and non-prescribed substances to try to retrieve that sense of well-being once again.

At the other end of the continuum, our bodies try to communicate what we interpret as "bad" feelings. To tell us there is something wrong—either outside or inside of us—our bodies give us clear signals through contraction, aches, pain, and heaviness. If we are willing to listen to the messages, we will catch on to what the tight shoulders, queasy stomach, clenched jaw, or low-grade headache is trying to tell us. Anger, sadness, shame, fear, and general unhappiness—all are our interpretation of a variety of degrees of the body squeezing in on itself. And once again, our physical sensations are the main way that our bodies have to tell us what is occurring emotionally for us.

Using the Inner Map

To understand how our Inner Map[7] works, start with a vertical axis of expansion/contraction. The more open you feel, the higher up on the scale you are; the denser your feelings, the lower down on the scale. At any point, you can tune in to your body sensations to find yourself somewhere on the continuum from more expanded to more contracted:

(feel "good" or "better")

More Expanded

More Contracted

(feel "bad" or "worse")

Even though it might be enough to just be aware when we are feeling expanded or contracted, we humans seem to enjoy making things more complicated. Look at the Inner Map to see how to locate yourself according to your body sensations. (See Appendix A for a more in-depth understanding of each of the emotional states.)

Locating yourself on the Inner Map can help you tell the difference between your expanded and contracted emotional states. We feel expansion in the open and enjoyable feelings of love and joy, contracted in the tight and less comfortable feelings of anger, fear, and sadness. When we tune in to how we feel from the inside when we experience these different emotions, we can start to see how they line up on a continuum of energy—from least energy (contracted) to most energy (expanded).[8] If you can remember a time when you felt ashamed, do you notice how you don't really want to move, how you might feel frozen? Now remember a time when you felt guilt: doesn't it have a little more energy than the shame did? We usually describe sadness with words like "heavy" or "low," but there is something about feeling sad that is not as contracted as feeling shame or guilt. With sadness we have a sense of something happening, of being able to move through our experience.

The emotions of shame, guilt, despair, and sadness are at the bottom of the Inner Map because they have the least energy in them. When we are feeling them, life seems dark. We might talk about feeling "dead inside," hopeless. Think about the language we use when we talk about these feelings, often using words that refer to what we would like to expel from our bodies (let's just list "pissy" and "crappy" here).

We feel more energy as we move up the states of the Inner Map, even when we are not yet feeling "good." You can see this in the difference between feeling fear and feeling anger: anger clearly has more energy within it. Some people prefer feeling the bigger energy of anger than feeling the lower energy of fear. On the other hand, some people like to feel fear over anger precisely because its lower energy feels easier to control.

As we continue up the axis, notice the line between the states that drain energy from us and those that energize us. Like the equator, this is an important boundary, one that will be useful to you as you are figuring out your bearings. Asking "Am I 'Above the Line' or am I 'Below the Line'?" will help you find out if you are having an emotion that feels negative—one that uses up energy—or an emotion that is positive—one that enlivens you. Once you have some awareness that your emotions either use up your energetic bank account or add to it, you may decide that it is worth the time it takes to shift yourself out of the less energizing emotions.

You can see why emotions associated with states like anger, fear, and sadness have a reputation as being negative: when we are in them, we are drawing from our reserves.[9] This makes sense from a survival perspective: each of these emotions is hardwired into our brains, ensuring automatic reactions to any perceived threats to our existence. Each reaction requires some sort of energetic outlay, which puts us into a dilemma: these negative emotions are essential to our survival, so we shouldn't avoid them, but there is a cost to being stuck in them. Being Below the Line—in survival mode—is equivalent to being in what can be called "Reactive Brain."

> *Bonnie really wanted to have a more positive relationship with her mother. She'd take deep breaths before her weekly phone calls, center herself, but it always seemed to happen: as soon as she heard her mother's exasperated tone, she felt herself tighten up, and before she knew it, she was once again arguing about the most ridiculous things.*

Reactive Brain is a world unto itself. Once we are in Reactive Brain, it is hard to get out; and once we are in it, it is likely that we will pull others in with us. Acting from those emotional states Below the Line—Shame, Guilt, Despair, Sadness, Fear, Anger, and Pride—is likely to start an energetic chain reaction. (You can find out much more about each of these emotional states in Appendix A.) One person's anger tends to spark someone else's fear, which then might lead to a defensive, angry response, and in turn the first person can become even more angry. Or being around someone's sadness could spark someone else's shame, leading to both people feeling drained and unhappy.

Once these pinballing cycles get started, it can be difficult to shift back Above the Line. Fear draws Anger—ping! Anger pulls for Anger—ping! Shame attracts Fear, which draws Anger, triggering Guilt—it can go on and on. Even if we manage to stay in a positive place for a few rounds of an interaction with somebody, the density of one person's being Below the Line can pull us under. Remember a time when you said just one wrong word to an intimate other and things seemed to just ricochet out of control? Or consider the conflicts of the Middle East. Reactive Brain is contagious.

Being in the area Above the Line, where emotional states energize us, is a completely different experience from being in the zone Below the Line. We intuit this when we describe emotions such as love and joy as being "positive"—these emotions increase our energetic bank accounts. In this zone, we are no longer just reacting instinctively to threats; we can draw on those parts of ourselves that can respond in a conscious, thoughtful way. Here we can notice that we might be repeating old patterns and choose to make different choices. Because we are calmer, we can think of innovative solutions and new possibilities. We are now in the area of "Creative Brain." Note the progression on your Inner Map and how there is an ever-increasing amount of energy from Willingness to Neutrality to Acceptance, Appreciation, Love, and finally Joy.

Note that the state that takes people across that imaginary border we call the Line is Willingness—the willingness to face into our own unconscious patterns and the willingness to see that we are creating the results we are getting. Crossing the border through this channel—letting ourselves be willing to see our unconscious selves—creates a huge shift in consciousness. Instead of viewing life as something we are "at the effect of"—that billiard ball that bumped into us and made us do what we did—suddenly we can see how our actions and our inner world create how we view and respond to reality. No longer at the effect of what is going on around us, we can take charge of how we respond and how we act.

Just noticing our own emotional state and wondering how we got into it can have monumental effects. The willingness to notice and wonder takes us over the line, shifting us into Creative Brain. This shift helps us feel better almost instantly. It also means that we move through the world with much more ease because we are not setting off reactions in others. Life flows as we feel energized by our Above-the-Line emotions, and we feel empowered by our ability to move toward our goals.

Hanging on to being right, being convinced of your position, believing your thoughts, are all signals that you are not willing and are all signs that your Reactive Brain is in control. There is nothing wrong with not being willing; you are just choosing to stay Below the Line. This is the moment of choosing between being right and being happy.

Gay Hendricks calls the state of Willingness "the gateway." Stay unwilling and you can access only what you have always known. Sail through your unwillingness and you suddenly move through a channel into possibility.

Willing to Be Willing

By the way, it is possible to *want to* be willing without actually *being* willing. Wanting willingness will not change anything, so let yourself wait until you experience true willingness. You will feel it in your body if you give yourself enough time and space. A powerful step to take when you feel unwillingness is to deliberately resist harder. Be even more unwilling. Let yourself fully feel the contraction of the energy, to be in a state of "No! I don't want to!" Some foot stomping and raspberry blowing can aid in this moment of whole-body resistance.

To nonjudgmentally notice your own resistance is like drinking an elixir that, over time, can create a "Yes! I want to!" And suddenly you will be ready—and willing. There's no rush; let yourself have your own timing.

Living in Creative Brain versus living in Reactive Brain is like the difference between sailing a ship with or without a rudder. Life in Reactive Brain means we are blown around by any storm, are vulnerable to the whims of the weather, and can't get where we want to go because we are too busy dealing with the obstacles in our way. Living in Creative Brain, however, means that we are free to choose where, in all the wide seas of life, we want to go. Storms will still happen, but we can use them as helpful information, feedback about our journey. In other words, when we live in Creative Brain, we are the captain of our life's ship.

To get a sense of the power of the emotional states Above the Line, try this: Imagine that you and your beloved have just had an argument and you are feeling stuck in anger. Even though your mind dishes up some really good reasons for why you deserve to be angry, eventually you notice you don't really like feeling this way. That is the pivotal moment: when you could just hang on to being right and keep feeling angry or you could decide to do something completely different. Can you see that from here it is a natural step into being willing to change your emotional state?

When you come through the channel of Willingness, the choppy waters subside into Neutrality, you take the tiller, and you steer into Acceptance. Now you can easily see creative solutions that were not clear to you before, and next thing you know, you feel more and more loving, joyful, and peaceful. We tend to feel better and better as we move up through these states. And again, notice our language. We feel more "open," we feel "up," we feel like we are "floating." Welcome to Creative Brain, the zone of the natural high! Not only do you feel better inside, but now you attract others who want to share the joy.

The State of Well-Being and Attractor Energies

You might be starting to see how powerful we are when we can influence our emotions. (Notice the word "influence" here. We have no *control* over our emotions; this is a mistake people often make, trying to shut down emotions in an attempt to get rid of negative feelings.) Now get ready for two more big impacts of our emotional states: how our emotions affect our sense of well-being and how our emotional states create "attractor energies."[10]

First, a person's thoughts and experiences of the world are completely determined by her or his emotional state. If someone feels fear, for example, his thoughts and experiences of the world will support his sense that the world is a fearful place. This is an important point: the fear state occurs first; the story that supports his fear follows. If he is angry, he will find evidence that justifies his state of anger. And if he is joyful, the world around him and the people in it look beautiful. This is a fundamental idea, particularly in relationships, which is why it is crucial that you learn to locate yourself on your Inner Map. Everything you perceive is filtered through your emotions. If you feel loving, you will perceive others around you—including your partner—completely differently than if you are angry. Your loving emotional state will lead to thoughts that support it; your anger will remind you of past experiences when you felt angry and will support your current anger. If you want to change your thoughts about the world around you and the people in it, you must first change your emotional state.

Most people believe just the opposite, that their thoughts are true, and—believing their thoughts—they try to control the people around them. If they have the thought "My boss is a jerk," their next action will result from that thought. They might stay distant from their boss, or complain to a co-worker, or think about getting a different job. Instead of realizing that their emotional state is creating their perceptions—and so using their energy to change their state—they fruitlessly put their energy into trying to control the world they perceive as real.

Look at what happens when they understand that their state is creating their thinking: They notice their thought, "My boss is a jerk," and the thought reminds them to locate themselves on the Inner Map, checking out their body sensations and realizing they are in the Fear state. Now that they know where they are on the Inner Map, they can shift to a higher level, say, Willingness. Now a new thought is available: "I'm willing to see what's really going on under the surface. I wonder what I'm not yet seeing about who I am in this interaction?"

There is another key consequence to being in a particular emotional state: the state itself creates "attractor energies" that draw particular responses from others. The person walking around in fear in the previous example will pull in negative responses from those around him, responses that are attacking, hostile, or otherwise supporting his notion that he does, indeed, have reason to fear others. It is like sending out a radio signal in a specific frequency that only certain listeners will tune in to or giving off a particular scent that only attracts one species of animal. Being in a certain state starts an ongoing feedback loop that not only supports staying in that state but also makes us believe that we are seeing the world accurately. In his book *Power vs. Force*, David Hawkins uses the example of how many ways there are to see a homeless person on the street, depending completely on one's own state: frightening, disgusting, a degenerate, just a regular person in need, a friend, or the divine itself.

This is a good place to slow down and take a breath. When you embrace the concept that your emotional state creates your experience of the world, you have the key to stepping into your full power. No longer are you at the effect of everyone around you. You can stop putting your energy into trying to control others in order to feel better. Instead, those you relate to become a mirror for your inner world, giving you information to help you locate yourself. Just as knowing your longitude and latitude is a necessary skill on the open sea, watching your thoughts, your sensations, and other people's responses to you will give you the bearings you need to find yourself on your Inner Map.

Below are two examples of how you and your partner might handle a typical relationship conflict. In the first, you believe your partner is responsible for the way you feel. In the second, you are taking responsibility for your own feelings.

Here is how it might look when you have the inaccurate perspective that you are at the effect of your partner: Maybe you are thinking, "I wish my partner would use a nicer tone when she talks to me." The old way would be to try to train your partner to use a different tone when speaking with you, to put lots of energy into this: "Can we agree that you won't talk like that to me ever again? I don't like it. It sounds like my mother sounded." Most partners agree to something like this, though it is a doomed agreement because they'll inevitably forget to do it, which will lead to your next complaint: "I thought we talked about this. You said you wouldn't speak to me that way anymore!" So then they say they will try harder. When they (of course) forget again, this will produce the ultimate: "You used that tone AGAIN. How can I trust you?! You're so RUDE!" As much as they try, typically those around us just aren't willing or able to be trained. Even if they want to remember your instructions, at some point they will be too tired or activated into their own old patterns to do so. So then you put your energy into trying harder to control them, which inevitably fails. Big energy drain, right?

Here is how it might look when you put your focus onto something you really have control over—you: You hear in your partner's voice "the tone." Instead of reacting, you check in with your body and notice that your stomach feels tight. As you stay with this feeling, letting it get bigger, you realize you are afraid, which locates you at Fear on your Inner Map. Breathing into your fear, you have the thought that you are afraid your partner doesn't love you anymore. You realize that as long as you stay at the Fear level, you will continue to be tuned in to scary things that might happen—like your partner leaving. In fact, you understand that while you are in the Fear state, you will keep attracting attacking responses from your partner that support your thought that she does not love you.

Pinpointing where you are on the Inner Map puts you at the helm. Instead of waiting for your partner to change, you can put your energy into something that has immediate and maximum effect: changing where you are on the Inner Map. (You will learn skills to shift your emotional states in Chapter 4.) You know that if you move up the axis from Fear, you can even go Above the Line from Reactive Brain into Creative Brain, and you will feel better, you'll view your partner from a more expanded place, and you'll attract responses from your partner that are much more positive.

This is a life-changing concept. It means you no longer perceive yourself as the victim of those around you. Are you starting to see what a difference this could make? It might take some practice to get the hang of it, but the more you practice, the more you will be able to steer where you want to go. Here are some examples of how this works.

> Tom was unhappy in his fifteen-year relationship. He went through the motions to be a good husband, but he didn't feel connected with his wife. Mostly he stayed busy at work, but when he woke in the middle of the night, his thoughts kept drifting to how unappreciated he felt for all he did for her and the kids and how he didn't even find his wife attractive anymore. Not like his colleague at work. She was hot. And she really liked him. It wasn't that bad that he was having an affair with her; at least he felt young again. And these darned backaches—he hated getting older. He planned to see a doctor about them—when he had time.

When Tom finally decided to locate himself on the Inner Map and find out what was really going on, he realized that he had been living Below the Line for years. His critical thoughts and backaches, as he tuned in to them, were indicators that he was feeling angry. He could see how his anger was keeping his wife at a distance. As he wondered into the anger, he began to see that none of this had anything to do with his wife. In fact, he could feel his life passing by, and he realized how his push toward success in the world was no longer fulfilling. Truly, he wanted to do something completely different. Facing into what was true for him motivated Tom to talk to his wife and gave him the courage to tell her the truth. He felt scared about her knowing everything that was really going on with him, but he knew it was time to start living authentically.

> Mary loved her partner of seven years, but she noticed she was no longer "in love." She figured this is just how relationship is, that romance always fizzles out eventually. She started staying up late and trolling through Internet dating sites. She even put together her profile, though she didn't yet have the nerve to post it. When Mary pulled herself away from the allure of trying to find a "new model," she sat herself down to locate herself. She tuned in to

her body, which she noticed felt tense. She especially noticed how heavy her chest felt, how that chronic cough seemed to start from a lump in her throat that—now that she noticed it—had been there for quite awhile. As she labeled her state as Sad, she started to see how many of her thoughts reflected that sadness: Her sense of giving up on real connection with her partner; her outlook on life that said it didn't matter what she did, nothing would change anyway—these verified how stuck she was in sadness. She realized she'd been staving off that feeling for a long time, ever since her favorite aunt had died the year before.

Getting Where You Want to Go

In order to locate yourself more precisely, let's look more carefully at what happens when we are in Reactive Brain. When we perceive danger, we go into an automatic response designed to activate us, commonly known as the fight-or-flight response.

Blood moves out of the neocortex—the analytic part of the brain—and into those parts of the brain directing automatic responses. Adrenaline and stress chemicals pour into the bloodstream, heart rate and blood pressure increase, muscles tense, getting "all systems go" so we can mobilize for a fight or run away. When you look at the Inner Map, you can see how activation increases from the lower-level states of Fear, on up to Anger, and finally to Pride ("I'm the King of the Forest!").

If the danger escalates and appears to threaten our survival, our bodies may react in the opposite way, freezing us into an automatic immobilized response. The body actually begins to shut down: thoughts stop, heart rate slows, we may even lose our ability to track what is going on cognitively—also known as dissociating. This state is similar to what happens to a mouse when a cat is playing with it: at some point, the mouse takes a "death-feigning" response,[11] the animal's preparation to be killed. The progressively less energy in the states Below the Line—Sadness, Despair, Guilt, and finally Shame—indicates that the body is shutting down. With each step lower on the Inner Map, it becomes more difficult to get the body moving again. When people have moved down to Shame, their thoughts may turn to suicide, in part because the lack of energy feels very close to death.

Reactive Brain is vital to our survival; it is not bad or something to try to avoid. Reactive Brain keeps us alive when a car barrels toward us and we quickly step back on the curb; it helps us prepare for a confrontation by tensing our muscles for a fight; and when a loved one dies, Reactive Brain functionally produces healing, gut-wrenching sobs. Our Reactive Brain doesn't think; our bodies take over so that we are ready to react. We have a million years of evolution to thank for such an elegant system.

However, there is a built-in problem with the Reactive Brain. Because it is to our body's advantage to stamp past experiences of survival threats into our memory ("DANGER! DANGER! NOTICE THIS!"), much of what it warns us about has nothing to do with the present. In other words, early experiences of threats to our physical and emotional being are coded into our brains, and our Reactive Brain does not distinguish between what is really a current threat and what is no longer relevant. Like a hidden alarm system, we will instantly pick up on and react to something in the present that reminds us of past threats to our survival. We don't have conscious control over this, which is a good thing because Reactive Brain is wired to react instantly to danger; however, we can notice when our nervous systems are activated and we are triggered into old patterns. We want to pay attention because when we are triggered, we are likely to act like the animals we are. And, following Hawkins' ideas about attractor energies, we may pull others into their own survival-oriented Reactive Brains.

That person previously described who had the thought "My boss is a jerk" is in Reactive Brain. When something happened, his body went into a fight-or-flight response; the boss triggered his Reactive Brain to remember—in his body—a time from his past when he felt threatened. He does not have to berate himself for this automatic response; instead, he can just notice and take steps to shift so that he does not engage his boss in a way that will draw her into Reactive Brain.

Let's revisit the idea that the mind makes up unreliable stories and the body's responses are reliable. Your body will always tell you the truth about your experience—with this caveat: it might bring your attention to unprocessed experiences you had in the past rather than tell you what is true in the present moment. In fact, if you notice that you are triggered into Reactive Brain, you can tune in to your body and ask if your reaction is about the present situation or if it has to do with some past event. The emotion that you tune in to will lead you back to the initial event that felt like a threat to your survival—if your mind doesn't talk you out of it.

One of the major contributors to conflict in relationship is ignoring that we are in Reactive Brain. Even though our brains are now in survival mode, we typically force ourselves to act as if we are fine. Unlike the Incredible Hulk, we don't turn green when we get triggered, so it isn't usually obvious to those around us. We look the same, yet our words might suddenly sound more anxious or aggressive. Though our outer demeanor may not show it, our hardwiring has pulled us Below the Line, which is immediately reflected by our defensive and negative thinking.

Suddenly others appear to be foes, not friends; our field of vision literally contracts as we try to figure out what is wrong so we can detect the threat; and our solutions are uninspired because they come from old, conditioned programming. The content of our thoughts reflects the level we have sunk to. And it is all automatic, part of the body's survival system.

Following Einstein's maxim that "no problem can be solved from the same level of consciousness that created it," we can see how being in Reactive Brain restricts our choices. Like one pool ball hit by another, our responses are limited by whatever emotional state we are in. You can test this by noticing the solutions your mind produces when you are in one of those states Below the Line. Rules, compromises, and the sense that "it's my way or the highway" all come when we insist on finding a solution while we are stuck in contracted states.

Moving from Reactive Brain to Creative Brain

Let's leave the nether regions of the threatened mammal brain and explore what it feels like to be Above the Line—that is, in Creative Brain. The movement out of Reactive Brain can occur when our body decides it is safe. Adrenaline has been metabolized, and heart rate and blood pressure return to normal. The brain can shift out of its narrow focus—on what is wrong and threatening—to move to an increasingly open focus, where we can now perceive the larger field of potential.

All that expanded energy allows for an entirely different set of solutions to come out of the fog. Where life in Reactive Brain means relying on old, timeworn, and often restrictive solutions, the shift into Creative Brain means that new possibilities are available. Put two Reactive Brains together and power struggles continue and life feels stuck and dull. Combine two Creative Brains and life feels playful and full of potential.

The movement up and down the Inner Map, through the different states Above the Line and Below the Line, usually happens unconsciously: we get triggered into the various states of Reactive Brain and then just find our way back into Creative Brain by relaxing, playing, or going to sleep. (Addictions are often our attempt to shift out of reactivity into creativity; unfortunately, they have a built-in rebound that can undo this effect.) The skill here is to notice what state we are in and then learn to consciously take steps to shift the brain out of Reactivity into Creativity to move up the states on the Inner Map. Each tool you learn in *The Relationship Ride* (and there are many to choose from) adds to your ability to take this empowering step.

Using Your Pressure Gauge

Let's add another instrument to your duffle bag, one to give you more precise map readings, no matter how hard the winds around you—and within you—are blowing. Like the gauges on a ship's boiler, your Pressure Gauge is designed to help you be more specific about what is happening in your body so you can make choices accordingly. It can be really helpful to know if your engines are running smoothly or if they are ready to blow. You have a good deal of information about what is going on when you are in Reactive or Creative Brain; now let's sort through that information so you can ultimately use your Pressure Gauge to fine-tune your ability to find yourself on the Inner Map.

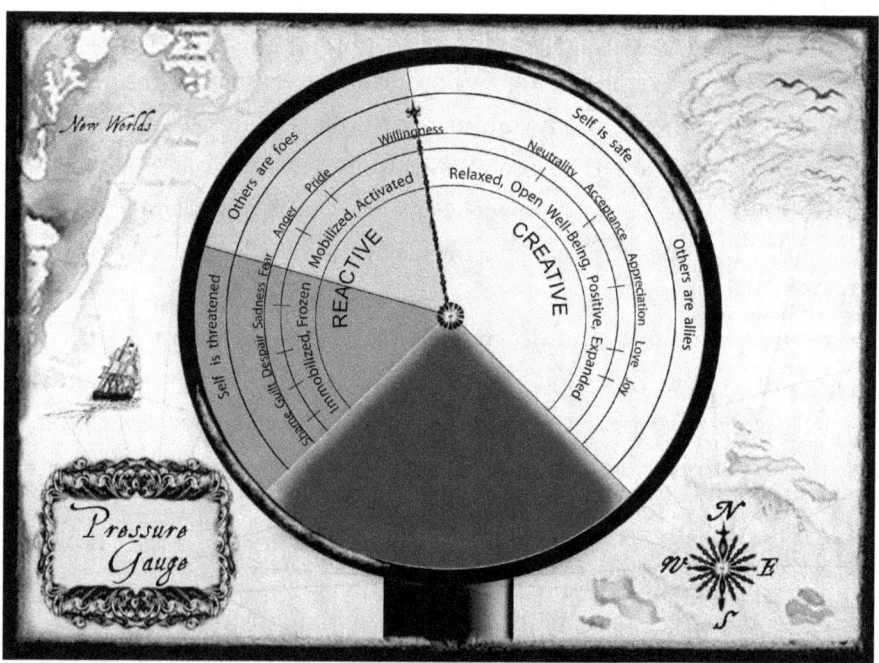

Can you see how these readings line up on the dials so that you can easily locate yourself as either running at full, creative steam or ready to blow?

Exercise 2: Locating Yourself on Your Inner Map and Pressure Gauge

Now that you have a sense of the vast territory available to you in your inner world, it is time to get out your Inner Map and use your Pressure Gauge to take some readings.

- Inner Map Reading:

  Locate yourself on the Inner Map, either Above the Line or Below the Line—that is, in Creative Brain or in Reactive Brain. This is the most important reading because it will lead to your next action. If you are Above the Line, you will find it easy to keep feeling better, like a balloon that just needs some gentle taps to stay in flight. If you are Below the Line, however, notice that it takes some effort to raise your energy. The lower you are on the Inner Map, the more exertion it takes to dislodge yourself from your energetic sludge.

- Pressure Gauge Reading:

  Now get out your Pressure Gauge to take more detailed readings of your physiology, emotions, thoughts, and the responses of those around you. Where are you located on your Pressure Gauge?

As you do this exercise, you might notice being in more than one state at a time. One part of your body (say your jaw) may be clenched from anger, while another (maybe your chest) could be heavy with sadness. Meanwhile, you could be curious about what is really going on. Taking this reading is simply a way to notice all that is going on in a moment. As soon as you have noticed your body sensations, they are likely to change anyway. Like the ever-shifting currents of the ocean, your body is an organic structure with a continuously fluctuating form, denoted by sensations that constantly change. Occasionally you may feel as if your emotional state is stuck in the shoals; however, by simply getting your bearings, you are taking an action that will get you moving again.

So how did it go? Can you find where you are on your Inner Map? Did the Pressure Gauge help?

Maps help us plan for our journey. And they help us find ourselves when we are lost. You can use your Inner Map to plot where and how you would like to live. Even more importantly, you can use it to find yourself when you have been blown around by the inevitable emotional storms that rise up in this exciting ride of life.

You can print a copy of the Inner Map from the Duffle Bag at www.JuliaColwell.com so you can carry it with you. It will come in handy. Knowing where you are is the first step in figuring out how to get where you really want to go.

Points to Steer By

- It is easy to get lost in the upheavals of emotional connection and expression that come with being in a relationship. Re-training ourselves to notice our bodies' messages is key to navigating through life.
- Our physical sensations are the main way that our bodies have to tell us what we are feeling emotionally.
- Asking "Am I Above the Line or am I Below the Line?" helps us find out if we are having an emotion that feels negative—one that uses up energy—or an emotion that is positive—one that enlivens us.
- Once we are in Reactive Brain, it is hard to get out; and once we are in it, it is likely that we will pull others in with us.
- The state that takes people over that imaginary border called The Line is Willingness, the willingness to face into the un-

known of our own unconscious patterns—and how those patterns are creating the results we're getting.
- In Creative Brain, life flows as we feel energized by our Above-the-Line emotions, and we feel empowered by our ability to move toward our goals.
- Everything we perceive is filtered through our emotions. If we want to change our thoughts about the world around us and the people in it, we must first change our emotional state.
- Because it is to our body's advantage to stamp past experiences of threats to our survival into our memory, much of what Reactive Brain warns us about has nothing to do with the present.
- Where life in Reactive Brain means relying on old, timeworn, and often restrictive solutions, the shift into Creative Brain means that new possibilities are available.
- The skill is to notice where we are and then learn to consciously take steps to shift the brain out of Reactivity into Creativity and so to move further and further up the Inner Map.

3

Getting Your Bearings: The Relationship Map

We are entering white water, nothing seems right. We don't know where we are, the water is green, no white.
~ Quote attributed to flight leader, Flight 19 designation of five TBM Avenger torpedo bombers that disappeared on December 5, 1945, over the renowned Bermuda Triangle

As you get a sense of the intricacy of finding yourself on your own Inner Map, you might begin to appreciate the exponential leap of complexity when you add in the Inner Map of another person. As you increase the depth of emotional connection with another, you become more and more affected by the internal world of the other person. A passing stranger's smile or grimace might flash through your body, producing an instant sense of warming or recoiling. A colleague's positive or negative mood in a meeting might stay with you (and the rest of your group) through the day, affecting your ability to solve a problem. Talking on the phone to a friend or family member who is happy or upset can influence you to feel open or to feel contracted. Raise the stakes to an intimate partner, and you find your world and his or hers to be undeniably woven together.

Connection is a contagious business. Our evolution as mammals has created an open loop system where others' emotional lives are designed to influence ours. Our very survival as a species has depended on our ability to elicit emotional responses from others. From a baby's cry to get his mother's focus because he needs to be fed, to a child's hysterical meltdown in the grocery store because she is exhausted, to an adult's fearful expression as an airplane is preparing to take off, our bodies have built-in systems to signal to those around us that we need their attention. Our faces are the only parts of our bodies where the skin is directly attached to muscle, demonstrating the importance of being able to signal to others what is going on for us emotionally.[12] Meanwhile, our culture tends to overvalue the ability to be on one's own. "Rugged individualism" has been a highly valued trait for Americans, to the point that we have spent the last twenty-five years accusing each other, and ourselves, of being "codependent." We are only now recognizing the importance to our wellbeing of physical and emotional connection with others. People who feel this contact with others—even with a dog or a cat—live longer, have fewer strokes and heart attacks, and are better able to handle life's stressors. From our body's perspective, our need for contact is as basic as our need for food.[13]

Seen from this angle, the problem is not that we are too dependent on one another; the problem is that we don't know how to connect in a way that supports thriving. In a relationship, it is easy to fall into ongoing cycles of triggering each other's Reactive Brain, which leads to feeling emotionally overwhelmed and ultimately shutting down. Now our quest is to create connection that allows each person to flourish in his or her separateness and create individuality that supports each to find a way to emotionally connect with the other.

Riding the Waves to Connection

Notice that this new information about our innate human need to have ongoing contact with others is a sea change in how we have viewed relationships over the last three decades. True emotional resilience comes from learning how to ride the waves through the Reactive Brain's activation so that we can melt into the soothing effects of another being's comfort.

When we place two Inner Maps side-by-side, we create a Relationship Map:

Because of the way human beings are designed, one person's emotional state will pull for a response from the other. This is called "limbic resonance," which is how the limbic system—the emotional center of our brain—draws in the limbic systems of others to a similar frequency. Intimacy between two people is like the resonance between guitar strings: the more intimate they are, the more their emotional states—their Inner Maps—influence each other. As frustrating as it might be to be influenced to this degree by those around us, it is just the way we're built. Consider your own experiences of coming into contact with a friend or your partner and how their mood affects yours. (You might not be quite as aware of how yours affects theirs.) In fact, it takes about fifteen minutes for two humans systems to come into synchrony.[14] This might explain why transitions from work to home are often the time when couples have a lot of difficulty reconnecting.

Comparing some different combinations of emotional states can give you a sense of how we can co-create the most blissful, exhilarating times with another as well as how we can get caught up in a resonance chamber of escalation, reactivity, and pure hell.

First let's look at how two Creative Brains might influence each other.

> *She feels loving. Her face is open, she looks right into his eyes, she feels safe. She moves toward him and says positive words that match how good she feels. He, in turn, moves toward her. His face is relaxed and he smiles. His pulse is normal and his body feels expanded. His tone and thoughts all reflect how good he is feeling. This positive energy reverberates between them in ever-expanding ripples. As they talk, they build on each other's ideas for the future, dreaming of possibilities that are far beyond what either one of them might individually imagine.*

Now let's look at two Reactive Brains in limbic resonance.

> *As she was leaving the office, her boss reprimanded her for making a mistake on a project she thought was completed. She feels agitated and stirred up. When she gets home and walks into the kitchen, he notices her tight mouth and shoulders, and he feels his muscles tense as he prepares for the inevitable.*
>
> *"Hi," she says, sighing as she puts her purse on the counter.*
>
> *"What's the matter?" he quickly asks, as he gets the wine bottle out and begins uncorking it.*
>
> *"Nothing's the matter. What's the matter with you?!" she retorts, plunking down in the chair.*
>
> *"Oh great, so this is how the evening's going to go. And I made us a nice*

dinner." He shakes his head and looks down, pausing before adding, "Jimmy's teacher called. She said he forgot to bring in the snack for today."

"FINE!" she explodes. "SO I'M SUPPOSED TO DO THAT, TOO! IN MY SPARE TIME!" She grabs her wine glass from him, gulping down half of its contents. He follows behind her, rolling his eyes before he takes his place next to her in front of the nightly news.

There are other possible combinations as well. Put a Creative Brain together with a Reactive Brain and the interaction could go either way, as the energetic question becomes who will be pulled up or who will be pulled down. This setup creates a tension between light and dark as expanded energy meets density; limbic resonance calls for one or both people to be affected.

Let's look more closely at the states of the Reactive Brain: Shame, Guilt, Despair, Sadness, Fear, Anger, and Pride. By themselves, these sound simply like the range of human emotions, what we all experience at some point in our lives. When you put them side by side with what is happening inside someone else, however, it becomes much easier to see how emotional states connect with one another. One person's anger might draw an angry response from another or perhaps fear or shame. Fear activates fear—or anger. Despair might trigger more despair—or anger. Overall, what specifically gets activated is unpredictable, depending on the conditioning of each person. Within intimate relationships, however, patterns are established that become the main dance of the partnership.

The Bermuda Triangle of Relationships

A specific pattern that shows up universally in any relationship—between individuals, within groups, or among countries—can be thought of as a Bermuda Triangle of limbic reactivity. Relationships can be lost to this zone as people sail around and around in it with no idea how to get out. Steven Karpman[15] formulated a simple and elegant map—the

Drama Triangle—to show how people get pulled into particular positions by their own and each other's Reactive Brain. Study this area of the Relationship Map carefully because this is where you are likely to get most stuck. Like a ship that has lost its rudder, sailing into the zone of the Drama Triangle means getting blown around by the whims of the Reactive Brain until you have completely lost your bearings.

Once you have stumbled into the Triangle, it is hard to resist the hypnotic pull to stay there. One Reactive Brain has the potential to trigger the next, until everyone has dropped Below the Line. And remember, the state that you are in creates your thoughts, so when you are in the dense states Below the Line, you'll believe that this is the only possible way to see reality. You'll spin stories about the other person's evil intent, how there is a right way and a wrong way to view reality (and yours is the right way, of course), how there really is something wrong with the other person, and how there is no way out. These illusions capture our attention, weaving a sense that the stories we tell ourselves—that is, our projections—are accurate, and because they are accurate, we should take them very seriously.

There are three entry points to the Drama Triangle: through the position of the Victim, the Villain, or the Hero.

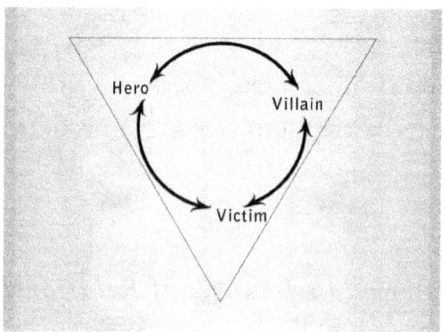

The figure above shows how each role depends on the others. A Villain must have a Victim, and both require a Hero to save the day. Similarly, the Hero needs someone to save—the Victim—and someone to save the Victim from—the Villain. A Victim needs a Villain to cower from and a Hero to be rescued by. These positions—so familiar to us through millennia of stories about evil sorcerers, the poor, down-trodden ones, and the brave champions who save the day—are at the foundation of every power struggle. People who are stuck in conflict have only to look Below the Line to locate themselves on the Relationship Map.

> Frank and Joan have been together for nine difficult years. They feel very stuck. Joan makes hostile comments about not being appreciated the way she used to be; Frank (who began the relationship by bringing Joan flowers and writing her love poems) mostly tries to stay out of the line of fire, placating Joan with promises he doesn't seem to ever follow through on because he secretly resents how demanding she has become.
>
> Both spend increasing amounts of time doing anything they can to feel better, including drinking alcohol, watching TV, and eating comfort foods. The dance goes on: Joan's Victim triggers Frank's Hero, but his rescuing attempts are now half-hearted because he really feels like a Victim, which in turn brings out Joan's Villain.

When we place all three Triangle roles on the Relationship Map, we can see something very interesting emerge. Notice that the Villain and Hero are aligned in the more energized area Below the Line; each has active and controlling energy. The Villain, whose main calling card is blaming others, uses anger and criticism to elicit shame in the Victim. Active energy feels more desirable to the Villain than the energy beneath the surface: fear of being out of control. Now we can see on the map that the Villain expresses anger while actually feeling fear.

The Hero—the good guy in the white hat—seems to be the polar opposite of the Villain—the bad guy in the black hat. However, if you look under the surface of what motivates the Hero—the need to "help"—you will find the same fear the Villain masks: being out of control. The Hero's fear is just as subterranean as the Villain's except that it is hidden under the veneer of "nice." Hero fear is less active, denser, and more contracted than Villain fear. The nice Hero can disengage from her own aggressive urges—and from her own fear—by helping.

The collapse of the Victim into helplessness indicates where his emotional state is on the Map. Victim fear is a frozen, non-moving fear, often with an unconscious disconnection from activating energy, perhaps as a learned response to not generate more anger from those around them. Thus the Victim tips free-fall into the lower realms of the Map, moving through Despair to Guilt and ultimately landing smack-dab in Shame.

The interaction of these roles is fascinating from an energetic perspective. The Villain's attack leads to the Victim's collapse—or does the Victim's collapse draw an attack from the Villain?

The Hero's activation to help allows the Victim to remain helpless; and the Victim's helplessness sends out a cry to be rescued that the Hero can't ignore. The battle between the Villain and the Hero is so compelling that our culture acts it out endlessly, from the mock battles of small children to athletic arenas to movies to politics.

The persistent reenactment of these roles in our culture is so ubiquitous that there must be a compelling reason that we are so drawn into them. Perhaps if we can understand what we get caught up in—that is, how our most primitive physiological structures fuel our roles in the Drama Triangle—we can find the route out. Before we look at what is happening in the body and brain of each individual in a relationship, let's look at how the epic struggle demonstrated in the Drama Triangle is mirrored in the animal world.

What Animals Teach Us about Human Behavior

In the animal world, mammal parents instinctively take care of their helpless babies while staving off a strong survival impulse to simply kill and eat them. Meanwhile, predators and their prey are caught in a primitive dance. The predator hunts down the prey and goes for the kill, while the prey, caught in the predator's jaws, instantly immobilizes into a whole system shutdown to get ready to die. One animal's aggression leads to the other's complete, pain-numbing collapse, all programmed by nature's eat-and-be-eaten plan.

There is another level at which our innate physiology takes over. As mammals, one of our most basic needs is to connect with another being. Our survival depends as much on emotional connection as it does on food. Babies demand their mothers' attention, falling into a physiological mess if they feel cut off from it. The mothering response is similarly programmed into all of us, males and females: nurturing another often stimulates hormones that fill us with the flush of love and protectiveness.

When we feel connected with another, our bodies relax into an inner world of safety that has facets of the Creative Brain. When we can't access this connection, we go into Reactive Brain, naturally moving into a state of loud protest. If this protest doesn't generate the response it is seeking, the final step is to drop into total despair. Look again at the Map and notice that the slippage from Anger and Fear down into Despair, Guilt, and Shame mirrors what happens when a being moves from the activation of demanding the ever-important contact to the shutdown of just giving up.

Since being Below the Line is the equivalent of being caught in mammalian survival instincts, it would make sense that, once Reactive Brain is triggered, humans are tossed into the undertow of our most primitive impulses. As we see or feel the signals of helplessness, we feel compelled to help and simultaneously disconnect from our own aggression. If our anger is activated, we might react like a predatory beast, attacking when we detect someone else's collapse. Finally, no matter how old we are, we can easily get triggered back to the most basic state of feeling dependent on others. This echo of our earliest experience of requiring protection and nurturing to stay alive leads us, at times, to give up expressing ourselves in order to receive it. Pulling ourselves into a submissive posture, shoulders hunched and eyes downcast, can lead to being taken care of. However, if our attempts to stay connected are blocked, we might collapse when our initial whine of protest doesn't work, and we finally just give up. All of these responses are intricately woven into a dance that feels like our very survival is at stake. Our bodies get more activated when we take care of another and become more passive when we are taken care of. And being caught in the Drama Triangle can take on the desperation of just trying to stay alive.

Let's go back to look at another place where these dynamics show up in the animal world—within the ranks of social hierarchy. Where there is ranking—for example, with dog packs and gorilla bands—we can see how different responses are appropriate according to an animal's rank. Alpha dogs are the most activated, displaying pride and anger; exhibiting fear would be viewed by the rest of the pack as weakness. For those further down the ranks, showing aggression would be to challenge the alpha, but the lesser-ranked ones do get to show the "weaker" energies of fear, despair, and even shame. Overall, the variety of emotional responses built into the mammalian system seems to be an elaborate way to keep social order.[16]

The animal pack relies on hierarchy to create safety and ensure survival by finding habitat and food. Social order can remain intact through this elegant system of most to least activation of energies. As humans, however, we must ask whether we want to continue to exist in the same realm as animals in survival mode. While these dynamics have led to our species lasting through millennia, they now are the setup for the power struggles that sink relation-ships. Hierarchy might give us an instinctive sense of safety, but it also creates the perfect setup for the Drama Triangle. To get out of Reactive Brain and back into Creative Brain, we have to find a new way to handle what is built into our brains by a million years of evolution. We must create a channel that is easily crossed between reaction and true power.

Moving Through the Channel to Creativity

How does this look? What does it take to move across a channel out of a million years of survival reactions and into the zone of creativity that is the emblem of fulfilling relationships?

When we understand how the Reactive Brain works, we can learn to steer ourselves into the channel that takes us from Below the Line survival mode into Above the Line creative mode by simply respecting our mammalian roots and taking care of our very basic need for emotional connection. When we understand that feeling connected with others is essential to our ability to function well in the world, it is easier to nurture our emotional ties by giving them plenty of time and attention. With this understanding, we would be sure to get plenty of skin-to-skin (or at least, clothing-to-clothing) contact with other warm-blooded beings. We would stop giving ourselves a hard time for wanting the comfort of contact with others. We would be willing to work hard at maintaining relationships rather than toss them aside during difficult times. We would be able to understand signals that humans use when we are threatened (loss of eye contact, muscle tension, numbing out) and take action to come back into contact, especially to stop debating issues and take action to re-create emotional connection. And finally, we would view the state of being "in love" not as something that inevitably dies out over time but as something couples can create anytime as long as they know how to shift back into the limbic resonance of two Creative Brains.

In Chapter 4, you will gain proficiency in the skill of moving through this channel between Reactive and Creative Brains. You will begin to understand that, to change your relationship, you need only to be willing to be aware of what is happening in your brain and your body. From that willingness, you can sail into the world of possibility.

Exercise 1: Contemplating the Relationship Map

- Download or print the Relationship Map from the Duffle Bag at www.JuliaColwell.com (or see the Relationship Map in Appendix A).
- Think of a current relationship issue in your life and locate yourself and the other person on the Relationship Map.
- Carry the map around with you, using it to get your bearings when you hit stormy seas with others.

Exercise 2: Stepping into the Drama Triangle

- Download or print the Victim/Villain/Hero pages from the Duffle Bag at www.JuliaColwell.com.
- Arrange them in a triangle on the floor.
- Exaggerate a current issue you are facing while moving from one spot on the triangle to another.
- Notice the sensations in your body.
- At what point do you notice being in Reactive Brain?

Points to Steer By

- Our evolution as mammals has created an open-loop system where others' emotional lives are designed to influence ours. Our very survival as a species has depended on our ability to elicit emotional responses from others.
- From our body's perspective, our need for contact is as basic as our need for food.
- Far from it being a strength to not "need" others, true emotional strength comes from learning how to ride the waves through the Reactive Brain's activation so that we can melt into the soothing effects of another being's comfort.

- The epic struggle demonstrated in the Karpman Triangle is mirrored in the animal world.
- When we feel connected with another, our body relaxes into an inner world of safety that mirrors the Creative Brain. When we can't access this connection, we go into Reactive Brain, naturally moving into a state of loud protest.
- Being caught in the Drama Triangle can take on the desperation of just trying to stay alive.
- While the dynamics of hierarchy have led to our species' lasting through millennia, they now are the setup for the power struggles that sink relationships.
- When we understand that feeling connected with others is essential to our ability to function well in the world, it is easier to nurture our emotional ties by giving them plenty of time and attention.
- The state of being "in love" is not something that inevitably dies out over time but is something couples can create anytime as long as they know how to shift back into the limbic resonance of two Creative Brains.
- To change your relationship, the only step you really have to take is to be willing to be aware of what is happening in your brain and your body.

4

Steering to Catch the Wind

To reach a port we must sail, sometimes with the wind, and sometimes against it. But we must not drift or lie at anchor.
~ Oliver Wendell Holmes

One of the most basic skills a sailor must have is an understanding of how to maximize the power of the wind. Think about it: you can't actually sail directly into the wind; this will completely stop your forward progress (known as being "in irons"). Instead, you must understand how to steer so that the wind catches your sails at just the right angle. Moving through the channel from Reactive to Creative Brain feels similar to when your sails lose their wind and your boat begins to drift with the currents—and that next moment of steering your ship to just the glorious spot where the sails fill and suddenly you're running full-speed ahead.

Choosing to move through the channel from Reactive to Creative Brain is what being conscious is all about. To be unconscious is to simply react according to one's conditioning, with no particular ability to choose something different. The body is exquisitely capable of moving through the world unconsciously, with one's implicit memory—all of the learned, mechanical responses—leading the way. Walking, catching a ball, typing on a computer would be arduous if we had to think about every micro-movement involved along the way. Once we have learned how to do something, we don't have to rethink our way through it.

However, the automatic nature of our actions implies that we have removed our awareness from them. This awareness allows us to move between levels of our brain. As soon as we notice what we're doing, thinking, feeling, speaking, we can see the effects of being who we are on the world around us, which allows us to truly make choices. Becoming conscious of our internal experience opens the door to shifting that experience instead of just drifting along through life. Les Fehmi, author of *The Open-Focus Brain*, says that to be truly powerful is to be able to choose where you place your attention.[17]

Researchers are converging in their ability to describe what occurs in the brain during the shift from Reactive Brain to Creative Brain. As with the parable of the blind men examining different parts of the elephant, and so believing the elephant to consist of a trunk or an ear or a very big foot, these descriptions sound different but are actually describing a similar phenomenon. Fehmi's "narrow objective focus" describes the state of the brain when it is in emergency response and how the body reflects this state by pouring out stress chemicals. He connects this narrow focus of attention with a certain pattern of brain waves called "high beta." He teaches people to shift into "alpha waves"—a relaxed and calm state—by learning to create a diffuse, open focus of attention. Eckhart Tolle, a master teacher of awareness, talks about a similar process, calling the shift back and forth the difference between "object consciousness"—the focus on the external, sensory world—and "space consciousness"—awareness of one's own consciousness interacting with the world.[18]

Temple Grandin, who has earned international respect for her ability to empathize with animals as the result of her work with her own autism, notices that, in brain research using Functional Magnetic Resonance Imagery, negative emotion and positive emotion light up different parts of the brain. This suggests that the density of being Below the Line (in Reactive Brain) is a different process than the expansiveness of stepping over the line (being in Creative Brain).[19] Others use the measure of "heart rate variability" to help people shift out of stressed states—when there is little variability in heart rate—into physiologically coherent, and therefore healthier, states.[20] Overall, it is clear that physical and emotional health are inextricably connected with our ability to shift into a higher level of consciousness, making learning these skills vital to the quality of our existence.

A paradox in learning these skills is that embodying them means they become automatic, yet to be conscious is to stay aware of what is really going on. The way through this paradox is to use your nonjudgmental noticing to observe both: your automatic, conditioned reactions as well as your presence—that is, your ability to simply be in the moment. Being open to *what is* without criticizing or comparing allows the light touch of awareness to keep you in the zone of being awake without clamping down on yourself, pulling you into contraction.

The specific moves you will learn in this chapter are all shifts into a more expanded level of consciousness. Imagine that you have an inner elevator: any one of these moves can take you up one or more levels. Or you might try their opposite and watch your consciousness plummet to the ground floor. One of the underappreciated benefits of being in a partnership or a close relationship of any kind is that we get an ongoing stream of potential triggers into Reactive Brain. Like a batter practicing with an automatic pitching machine, relationship gives us a never-ending flow of opportunities to go into Reactive Brain and then decide to make our way back to Creative Brain.

As you begin to use these tools, understand that they are similar to throwing yourself a life preserver as you feel the pull to go down, down, down the states of your Inner Map. The tools don't rely on an intricate communication technique that is easy to forget when you are in Reactive Brain. In fact, with one exception (Speaking the Unarguable Truth), there is little actual talking involved. Instead, shifting is simply about waking up and becoming aware: that you have gone into an old pattern, started reacting, are on automatic, drifting.[21] Like a sailor who has gone to sleep on watch, shifting is about coming to so you can adjust the sails and steer through whatever life has put in front of you.

It's time to lay out your duffle bag and fill it with all kinds of powerful and effective tools.

Shift Tool #1: Noticing

You first learned about noticing in Chapter 2 when you became aware of body cues that helped you locate yourself on your Inner Map. Noticing sounds simple: just tune in to your body's sensations and read the sensations as signals to how you are feeling. And yet using this move can be challenging. Your mind wants to keep you away from your body; it prefers to tell a story. Instead of focusing on the tension in your stomach and realizing you are scared, your mind might say, "See! You never should have trusted him! People—they'll take advantage of you if you're too nice." Or your brain might even dismiss what your body sensations are telling you: "I'm not scared. There's nothing to be afraid of." Humans love to make up stories, and a good story always includes judgment about something. Your challenge is to stay nonjudgmental, which requires just the facts, no embellishment. Just notice: "My stomach feels queasy" or "My stomach is in a knot" or "My stomach tingles with bubbles of energy." All of these are descriptors that, since you're the one feeling them, you could swear to; in short, unlike our unreliable stories, what you are feeling in your body is the truth.

Remembering to simply notice your inner world will keep you in your own experience, and being in your own experience means that you are facing into *what is*, a state that many of us will spend most of our life trying to avoid. We don't necessarily want to know that we're angry with our friend or sad about leaving or feeling sexual about someone who isn't our partner. Our mind and our body are often at odds about what we believe to be appropriate or acceptable. In fact, much of emotional conflict happens at that moment of shifting our attention away from what is happening. We often prefer to feel "anxious" rather than to know we feel afraid or angry, to feel "depressed" instead of grieving, or to treat physical symptoms rather than tune in to the emotions underneath the symptoms. Noticing what is true—what our body tells us—allows us to land in this moment, which is where all the action is.

Exercise 1: Noticing

Notice *what is* right this moment. Close your eyes and find five sensations in your body.

Shift Tool #2: Being Present

After we notice our body sensations, the Shift Tool of Being Present can take some additional effort, but it is powerful in its ability to fully use the energy within us. Letting our attention wander distractedly to the outer world versus placing it fully on what is going on in our body is the difference between a lighthouse beam sweeping across the sea and having it stop and aim its light directly into the anchored boat. The act of focusing our attention itself creates expanded awareness.

Our attention is a powerful energy; just ask your child, partner, or pet. When we focus our attention internally, we create space. Try it right now: Focus inwardly on a sensation somewhere in your body. First take an inner snapshot of its location and what it feels like. Now beam your attention on those sensations. Keep breathing while you are doing this, aiming your breaths at the sensations. What is happening now? Has the sensation changed at all? Do you notice more space?

Attention as an agent of change is the power behind being conscious. Attention brings us into the only place where anything is happening—right now. It allows us to become partners with our bodies to actually shift our sensations. Nonjudgmental attention creates space; this space allows us to expand our consciousness, moving us out of the solidness of form and into the boundless energy of potential.[22]

Many of us will do anything to move away from our emotions, keeping ourselves distracted through an endless variety of diversions—surfing the Internet, talking to friends, using drugs and alcohol, watching TV—anything to keep from feeling the depths of our emotional reactions. Life can pass us by as we think about the past or anticipate the future, as we think about anything but being here, right now. In *The Power of Now*, Eckhart Tolle describes the tendency to be anywhere but here when he says, "Most people treat the present moment as if it were an obstacle that they need to overcome. Since the present moment is Life itself, it is an insane way to live."[23]

There are many ways to train ourselves to keep our awareness in the present. Dancing, walking, singing, even an activity like rock-climbing that requires a single-pointed focus—all can provide a pathway into becoming more present. Meditation is another method that lets us develop this muscle. It is the practice of being present by bringing attention into the moment, over and over and over. Like a puppy, our mind wants to run around and chew on whatever it finds. By meditating, we can learn to train the puppy to come into stillness, to simply be with what is. If you have been around a dog that is calm, relaxed, and alert, you can appreciate the ability to respond that comes with being fully present.

Exercise 2: Being in This Moment

- To land fully in this moment, start by taking long, deep breaths.
- Watch what it is like to breathe, to notice your lungs expanding and contracting, your breath moving in and out of your body.
- When you have a thought, simply notice it and bring your attention back to your breath.
- You could do this for a minute, or for an hour, simply watch-

ing where your attention goes and bringing it back to your breath.
- Notice how your mind quiets and your body calms with this practice.

Shift Tool #3: Speaking the Unarguable Truth

This Shift Tool is the only one that requires verbal communication. It's a simple move, but beware: When your mind gets involved, this move might seem complicated.

Speaking in an unarguable way is simply putting two Shift Tools together—Noticing and Being Present—to describe to people around you or to yourself what is going on in your inner world. Typically, when our minds are in charge, we tell stories, and stories are always arguable:

- You don't care.
- It's always like this.
- Change is hard.
- People are wonderful / awful / beautiful / ugly / scary / helpful / bad / good, or ruining the planet.
- I can't do it. I'm overwhelmed. I'm not adequate / enough / a superstar / destined for success.

How do you know if you are saying something arguable? Simple: someone can argue with you. It is not about whether what you are saying is "true" or whether anyone would agree or even if it's supported by statistics: you are saying something arguable when what you are saying can be argued with.

What is unarguable is all about what is going on within your body, and that's a short list:

- Sensations
- Emotions
- The inner knowing of what you want/don't want

- Noticing what thoughts or images your mind is churning out

When you describe your body sensations or emotions, or when you say what you do or don't want, you are making statements that cannot be argued with:

- My stomach is queasy.
- I feel sad.
- I don't want to spend time with your family.
- My shoulders feel tense and my jaw hurts.
- I am so full of joy I want to sing. La-la-la!
- I'm having the thought that you don't love me.

You have been getting practice describing your sensations. See how they are unarguable? It is unlikely that anyone will have anything to say about you describing the rush of aliveness through your body, or the tightness in your chest, or your nausea. Describing sensations can seem really elementary, but doing so creates a clear pathway out of power struggles and stuckness.

Taking the step from noticing sensations to understanding what they are communicating—that is, our emotions and what we want/don't want—can be tricky because it can be difficult to accurately relate our bodily sensations to our emotions. Getting used to this language, however, will allow you to build your competence in connecting sensations with emotions and what you want.

There are two key ground rules in the land of the unarguable truth:

- Anyone gets to feel anything anytime for any reason.
- "Because I want to [or don't want to]" is the best reason there is.

These two ground rules cut down on conflict. In these examples, notice how speaking what is arguable immediately triggers Reactive Brain.

- Arguable:

    Person 1: Why are you mad? I didn't mean to hurt your feelings.
    Person 2: Well, of COURSE I'm mad. Who WOULDN'T be mad, you louse!

- Unarguable:

    Person 1: Why are you mad?
    Person 2: Because I feel mad. My jaw is tight and my pulse is racing.
    Person 1: Oh.

- Arguable:

    Person 1: Why do you want to leave the party? We just got here!
    Person 2: I hate these people! They're your friends, not mine. They're so shallow. They don't like me anyway.
    Person 1: Well, sure they like you! And who are you calling shallow! Maybe you're the shallow one!

- Unarguable:

    Person 1: I want to leave the party.
    Person 2: Oh.

For the sake of simplicity and to elude the ever-present tentacles of the mind, try using just five primary emotions to state what is true: mad, sad, scared, glad, and sexual. Sticking with these five can keep you from drifting into making arguable statements. These five emotions are like primary colors: they form the base for a range of more complex feelings. For example, when we feel "disappointed," we might actually be feeling a combination of sad and mad; feeling "frustrated" is really just one hue of mad. Many times our descriptions of our emotional world—such as "kind of nervous" or "fine, just tired" or "confused"—are really ways to stay out of our actual emotional experience. ("Sexual" is not typically considered one of the basic feelings. It is added to the list to remind people that we get to feel anything anytime for any reason, even sexual feelings. That means we can feel sexual whenever we feel sexual, not just with our partner.)

Here is a brief shorthand to understand how your body tries to communicate emotions:

- Fear typically expresses itself through tightness in the stomach and a desire to flee.
- Sadness can feel like an aching heaviness in the chest and heart areas or a lump in the throat.
- Anger, that "fight" impulse, might be a tightening of the arms, shoulders, neck, jaw, and lower back.
- Gladness can feel like spacious energy anywhere in the body. It is often centered in the heart area and may feel like a spreading of warmth through the chest.
- Sexual may be focused on the genitals, but it may also be delicious sensations anywhere in the body.

We often confuse what we are really feeling, especially anger and fear. The way to circumvent our stories about what we should be feeling—like, it's better not to be weak with fear or mean with anger—is to start with the sensation and then simply wonder what emotion best resonates with that sensation. Notice the contraction and specificity of those emotions that exist Below the Line (Sad, Mad, Scared) and the expansiveness of the Above the Line emotions (Glad). Sexual is also an expanded state.

Speaking the unarguable truth about emotion will sound like this: I notice [body sensations]. I feel [mad / sad / glad / scared / sexual]. For example: "I notice my jaw is tight. I feel mad." Or "I notice my stomach is in a knot. I feel scared."

However, beware of a common pitfall that can happen with using this language. People make statements like this: "I feel like you just don't understand me." Saying "I feel" in front of an arguable statement does not make an unarguable statement valid. "I feel that" or "I feel like" are *thoughts*, not feelings. An unarguable statement is this: "I feel," followed by an emotion—mad, sad, scared, glad, or sexual.

When you have thoughts, declare them as such. The mind is a master at making up stories (also known as projecting); it is from these stories that we are apt to start arguments. "I have the thought that you are a slob" or "I'm making up a story that you are a slob" makes it clear that you know you're in the grip of Storyland. Then it is just a short step to going back to what is unarguable, which would look like this: "I'm making up a story that you are a slob. And the truth is that I'm really just scared my parents are going to be critical about our home when they visit."

The final challenge of speaking the unarguable truth is to make the *whole statement* unarguable. So saying, "I feel tightness in my jaw. I'm angry" is a good start. But if you add "because you were late!" you can predict the other person's response: "I wasn't late; I said I'd be here *around* six!" How can you tell if your statement was arguable? If the other person can dispute your statement. The unarguable version would go like this: "I feel tightness in my jaw. I feel angry because I didn't get what I want!"

The main reasons for using the unarguable truth are to avoid blaming and to take full responsibility for one's experience. That is pretty straightforward with fear and sadness but can be more difficult with anger. Anger is like a heat-seeking missile: it wants a target. Staying unarguable with anger means sticking with the two reasons we get angry:

- Because we don't get what we want.
- Because we get what we don't want.

Using either of these statements means we don't need to make excuses or to make a case for our own experience. Here is an example:

Arguable:

"I've been thinking about going to see your family at the holidays and I think I'm going to have to work that whole time so I won't be able to go, plus we don't have the money for me to take the time off."

Unarguable:

"I don't want to go to your parents' house."

No reasons are needed.

We get angry because we perceive ourselves as being thwarted (not getting what we want) or being intruded upon (getting what we don't want). Inserting these reasons into talking about our anger will keep the statement unarguable. In the example about someone coming in late, notice how getting clear about being thwarted shifts the statement out of blame into taking responsibility for one's experience.

The unarguable truth is the shortest distance between your body sensation and how you express it. In the crucial moment of moving away from or back into wholeness, simply speaking *what is*—and, of course, feeling it—takes you right back to your essential self. Gay Hendricks calls honesty "the best sleep aid and aphrodisiac there is." Stories, distance, contracted body sensations disappear. Speaking what is unarguable can work like magic in quickly shifting a stuck conflict into an easy-going, connected interaction.

Exercise 3: Creating Unarguable Statements

Change the following statements from arguable to unarguable (key is at the end of this chapter):

1. You don't love me.
2. You're always late.
3. If we go that way, the traffic is going to be terrible.
4. I'm a loser.
5. Your tone sounds critical.
6. We don't have the money for that.
7. You don't ever want to touch me.
8. Our house is a wreck!

Shift Tool #4: Wondering

Wondering allows us to fully harness the power of the wind to fill our sails. Wondering opens us to "beginner's mind," the open field of consciousness highly prized by many spiritual traditions. It is the link to possibility, to the unknown, to the potential that is a step beyond what already *is*. As such, wondering is the first step to creativity.

Do you want to know what kills the state of wondering?

Being right. Being right requires a narrow focus of analyzing that leads our brains to look for what is wrong. Being right starts us on a chain of being critical and judgmental. When we insist that we know how things should be or decide that our picture of a solution is the only way, we stamp out the ember that, with some gentle blowing, could become the fire that lights up a whole new way.

Many relationships live (and die) on the question of who is right and who is wrong. People's opinions take on an almost sacred status.

"We should have a budget."

"We should be having more sex."

"You shouldn't use that tone with me."

"No, it wasn't last *Wednesday*; it was last *Tuesday*!"

"I can't believe you bought that brand! Don't you ever read the label?"

Arguments over who is right and who is wrong take on a tone of good and bad so that losing an argument really becomes an issue of losing face. This whirlpool of right/wrong, good/bad drains away the sense of well-being couples have accumulated as relationship capital.

Giving up being right can be a really big deal, so take a moment to enjoy it one last time. Say it out loud and let yourself land in the solidity of that experience.

I AM RIGHT!

Was that long enough? You want to do it again? Take all the time you'd like because that's pretty much all you get out of being right.

Now, are you ready to try something that might be more fun?

Wondering and being curious connect us to a part of the brain that provides us with a sense of well-being.[24] When we wonder, we are open to the idea of not knowing, and we may even feel an overtone of marveling at what could be. Stepping out of what we think we know into the world of possibility allows life to take on a sense of excitement. Being willing to wonder creates a pathway to answers we might never have thought to seek.

Exercise 4: Opening to Wonder

Gay and Katie Hendricks suggest beginning a good wonder with a satisfying "Hmmmmm." Try it now, a low, vibrating hum, and notice what that feels like in your body. You are tuning the instrument of your body for some creative, expansive thinking.

Ask yourself some questions, big questions that will open up your thinking and give you a sense of possibility:

- What don't I know about who I am?
- What do I really want?
- What does real space feel like in my body?
- How am I creating this issue?
- How am I keeping this issue going?
- What do I have to learn from this situation?

Write down some of your own wondering questions. How does it feel to be open to wonder?

Shift Tool #5: Breathing

This Shift Tool is pretty basic. If you can't remember to do anything else, taking a deep breath will fill your sails. When we are in Reactive Brain, we automatically shift into fight-or-flight breathing. Our breath is shallow and high in our chests. Try it right now: Take some rapid, quick breaths, and be sure to move only your chest. If you keep doing this, you will actually induce a state of anxiety. Because we have conscious control over the typically automatic process of breathing, deciding to slow down and deepen our breaths will have a direct impact on shifting our overall physiology out of threatened reaction and into a state of calm and safety.

Focusing on your breathing is an instant way to shift from a focus on the external world to a focus on the internal, thereby instigating the other shift moves, like Noticing, Being Present, and Wondering.

Exercise 5: Learning to Breathe

Changing your breathing as a Shift Tool may not impress your mind as having much power, but don't listen to your thoughts.

Instead, do some experiments.

- When you notice that you are in Reactive Brain, place your hands on your belly and breathe deeply and slowly, watching as your hands move with the rhythm.
- Do this for at least a minute.
- Now notice how your thinking has changed.

Shift Tool #6: Moving

When boats are stuck in irons—that is, they are becalmed—they need paddles or oars to help them get moving again. Bodies aren't very different from this. Our inner stuckness tends to be reflected by our body's unwillingness to move around. Becoming an adult (at least in Western cultures) seems to include reducing our body's movements so that we often sit still or move only in linear ways, walking straight toward our goal, not deviating from the norm. When we are in Reactive Brain, we reflect the Below-the-Line state we are in by clenching our fists in Anger, freezing our whole body in Fear, or collapsing over our solar plexus in Shame.

Moving allows us to consciously interact with our body to shift to a different state. We can unclench our fists or loosen our limbs or expand our chest. Moving can be especially effective when we have gone into a freeze response. Remember that when we freeze we are in Reactive Brain, so moving might feel counterintuitive. Our mind will tell us it really is a bad idea to move at all, but, as we learned in Chapter 2, our mind tends not to be trustworthy when it comes to giving us objective information about the state we are in. Choosing to move can feel like taking a leap of faith into the space between Reactive and Creative Brains, where simply moving any area of the body can feel dangerous. But that movement will allow the body to experience a new state and open the possibility of further shifts.

Exercise 6: Moving

Play with movement right now.

- If you're sitting, experiment with making your body more still, then with starting to move different parts of your body—twirling your finger, clenching and unclenching muscles, wrinkling and unwrinkling your brow.

- Do you notice a change in your sense of well-being?
- If you really want to shift, get up, play some music, and DANCE!

Shift Tool #7: Playing

When you are feeling stuck, playing is probably about the last thing you want to do. In fact, your Reactive Brain will probably actively protest against you doing such a thing. The survival orientation of being in Reactive Brain means that life seems to be very serious indeed, and people who are playful just don't understand what is really going on. As Katie Hendricks often says, "If you have the thought 'It's not funny!' you know you're in the grip [of Reactive Brain]." Because it is impossible to experience emotional distress and emotional uplift[25] at the same time, choosing to play is like pulling the switch on a railroad track: it can take a little effort, but once you've done it, you'll be heading off in a new direction.

Temple Grandin makes the point that mammals don't need the neocortex to play, and in fact, this "advanced" part of the brain can really get in the way of having a good time.[26] The neocortex wants to analyze, judge, and critique, which makes it excellent at mathematics, physics, and accounting and not so good at having fun. Without the ability to play, however, we lose our ability to creatively solve problems. And our lives can seem dull, flat, and colorless.

As we will find in Chapter 6, moving through emotions requires that we express them. To play is to create an endless variety of expressions, being in the moment-to-moment connection from our inner selves to the outer world.

For those of you thinking, "Well, count me out—I'm not creative, and I'm NOT interested in playing!" please reconsider. Here's the thing: It is impossible *not* to be creative. Even if you just sit there in one place for the rest of your life, you are creating *that* expression: Let's call it "Still life on a chair." Once you get up, you have to decide which direction to move. That is you expressing in a creative way.

As you become more comfortable with this idea that you are the one behind every move you make—all of the choices that reel out and become your life—you can begin to observe how you are the creator of your existence. You are no longer reacting—you're responding. You're bringing *you* into life, your real self, not just your conditioned self. This is how life *becomes* play: every time you make a choice to follow your impulse—any impulse—you're playing. And the juicy new question you could be asking is, "How could I be enjoying myself more right *now*?"

Exercise 7: Playing

Give yourself five minutes (though once you try this, you might want to extend that time to an hour, an afternoon, or a day).

- Sit still until you have an impulse. It could be to shift in your chair or to scratch your nose.
- When you have the impulse, follow it. Then wait for the next impulse—and the next—until you're simply creating a chain of following the next surge of energy that your body produces.
- As you tune in to what your body is telling you it wants to do, notice how similar or different your activities are from what you would typically be doing.

Shift Tool #8: Making It Bigger

There is an energetic principle that says, "What we resist persists." This notion is essential to the idea of shifting because resisting *what is* seems to be part of the human condition. Part of us just does not want to have the feeling, do the work, be aware, and this part of us feels comfortable with the familiarity of contraction and density. The Shift Tool of Making It Bigger is an effective way of countering our tendency toward lethargy and sticking with the status quo. It's simple: Whatever is happening for you, exaggerate it. If you notice yourself resisting, let yourself complain in a loud, whiny voice about how IT ALL IS REALLY, REALLY HARD. If you feel anxious, let your whole body shake, your voice quaver. If you're down in the dumps, really get into the drama of how terrible everything is: close your drapes, wrap yourself up in a blanket, watch depressing movies. If you're angry with your partner, exaggerate your anger by jumping up and down, wagging your index finger, making faces. You might notice how suspiciously close to playing this becomes so that your resistance might just melt away while you're not looking.

Exercise 8: Making It Bigger

- Whatever posture you're in right now, exaggerate it. If you're slumping, slump more. If you're sitting up straight, see if you can get even more rigid.
- Take this out into your day, making some posture, expression, or experience bigger.
- Watch the shift in your energy.

Shift Tool #9: Expressing Creatively

You can probably see how there has been a progression of Shift Tools, from the most subtle—Noticing and Being Present—moving into the increasingly active—Speaking the Unarguable Truth, Wondering, Breathing, Moving, Playing, and Making It Bigger. All of these Shift Tools are ways to creatively express your experience as opposed to simply reacting to your experience. You can take these shifts even further, however, so that your life becomes an ongoing creative expression of your internal world. Then you are constantly in that zone between experience and expression, the ultimate in staying conscious.[27]

Expressing creatively is infinite in its variations. It can be more formal expression, such as journaling, writing poetry, telling stories, playing music, or painting, drawing, dancing, or sculpting your experience.

Or it can be informal, like deciding to use a different voice tone or sing your experience or express it in a made-up language or sculpt it in air. Who knows what you might come up with in the moment, what image you decide to convey or noise you might make that would exactly match what is going on in your inner world. Letting yourself express *what is* allows those of us outside of you to truly understand who you are on the inside in relation to what is happening on the outside.

Exercise 9: Expressing Creatively

- Tune in to your body sensations.
- As you notice what is happening in your body, try out different kinds of expressions. You could match the sensations with a sound or a movement; you might write down words that describe them, or write a quick haiku or poem about them. You could journal about whatever your thoughts are about your current experience or draw a picture. Maybe you'll put on music that has a similar feel or rhythm to your sensations; you might dance to the music.
- Try out different types of expression; notice how your sensations shift as you express them.

Shift Tool #10: Appreciating

Appreciating is one of the most powerful and rapid Shift Tools of all. While seemingly a simple process, choosing to appreciate creates a variety of physiological changes. Our visual focus moves out of a narrow state of looking for what is wrong and shifts into a more pleasurable state of being diffuse and open. Our heart rates move into what is known as "coherence," a rhythm that is associated with ease and inner well-being.[28] Our internal state becomes something akin to what people have defined as being connected with God, spirit, or Source.[29]

The act of appreciating is about being "sensitively aware" of whatever your focus is on, with an objective of seeing the positive.[30] We make a *choice* to appreciate, and we can appreciate anytime, anywhere, just by deciding to. Try that right now: Look around and ask yourself what you appreciate. If your answer is "nothing," try harder. Maybe your brain is in a state of looking for what is wrong. Most of us have been trained to find what is wrong; many, such as accountants, designers, doctors, repair-people, psychotherapists, and attorneys, actually earn a living by detecting where the problems are. So shifting your attention to what is right could require developing some new muscles.

Try it again: What do you notice that you could appreciate right now? It might be the chair you're sitting in and becoming aware of all of the people it took to design the chair, find the materials, build it, ship it across the country, and get it to the store. Let your attention open to whatever else in your life you can appreciate right this minute. What's that like, to shift to this state of appreciation? Have you found your way up the Inner Map to feeling more expansive?

Exercise 10: Appreciating

Deciding to live in appreciation is a powerful commitment. There can be a lot of social support to focus on what is wrong in the world, to join the cacophony of cynics and complainers. Try living in appreciation for just an hour to see how it feels. If you like living in appreciation, increase the time to another hour and then another. Maybe you can handle a whole evening, a day, or a weekend. At some point, you might notice that you can maintain an appreciating approach for much of your life. As you make this shift, you might want to track how else your life opens up for you—living in appreciation is equivalent to your sailboat "running before the wind," living with the wind at your back, pushing you along with no effort at all.

Shift Tool #11: Speaking What You Really Want

Getting clear about what you really want and then being willing to speak it is about how to steer your life, and this is such a crucial skill that it takes a whole chapter to do it justice. We will delve into creating and speaking what you want in the next chapter.

Bonus Shift Tool: Loving What Is

As you become increasingly adept at appreciating *what is*, you can turbo-charge this positive state by adding this next energy: *loving what is*. Appreciation allows you to jump Above the Line by focusing on the positive; choosing to love your experience will zip you even further up your Inner Map to expanded states that support magic happening in you and around you.

We intuitively know how love can change things for the better. Our culture is filled with references to "the power of love." And as the Beatles told us many years ago, "All you need is love." We get confused, however. We use the word "love" in the context of loving a person so that saying "I love you" can become a casual line. As a conscious Shift Tool, *love* is about the action of loving: in this case, love is a verb, not a noun.

Bonus Exercise: Loving What Is

Try it now.

- Think of someone or something you love easily.[31] The important word here is *easily*; partners often aren't the best choice for this exercise because of complicated emotions that can get in the way of truly seeing them. You might want to think about a beloved child or pet, or a beautiful piece of music, or a special place. Think of something or someone that immedi-

ately creates a sensation in your heart that resonates with love.
- Let your attention stay with this person, animal, or place, or whatever you chose.
- Breathe into the sensations you feel. Let them get so big that they fill your whole chest, then your torso, then your whole body.
- Marinate in these sensations of love.
- Now, as you continue to feel these sensations, think about your life. Maybe there is a circumstance that is worrisome or difficult or maybe all is well. Either way, turn your loving attention on *what is* and watch your experience of it expand.

Phew! That duffle bag of yours must be heavy by now. And every one of the tools you loaded into it will come in handy when you are out on the open sea. Storms, sand bars, getting into the doldrums—every possible circumstance that puts you into Reactive Brain can be dealt with using these powerful methods.

Choosing to Be Conscious

No matter how sweet the sailing, you will inevitably find yourself drifting, either unaware that you have gone unconscious or unwilling to do anything about it. It's tempting to use drifts instead of shifts, as they tend to provide momentary relief from the contraction that we are experiencing. Drifts take us off course from our bigger intentions in life as we give in to the short-term gratification of moving away from what doesn't feel good while ignoring the long-term consequences of our choices.

Human beings are creative in the ways we choose to drift; we each have our favorite ways. Do you see in this list your preferred methods to go unconscious? Do you have any to add?

- Indulging in addictions (nicotine, alcohol, drugs, sugar, exercise, Internet, TV, gadgets, video games)
- Being right or being wrong.
- Organizing
- Cleaning
- Controlling others
- Self-loathing
- Staying busy / overworking
- Holding an argumentative position
- Staying serious
- Staying in the story
- Believing limited thoughts
- Daydreaming
- Going foggy
- Defending
- Distracting
- Obsessing
- Freezing
- Avoiding
- Withdrawing
- Dominating or submitting

Do any of these drifts sound familiar? Jot down your particular favorites.

It is possible to consciously drift. It is the equivalent of giving up the tiller, dropping the sheet connected to the sail, and drifting with the wind and the currents. Giving up responsibility for your life can momentarily feel like you are lightening your load—that is, until you look around and notice that you have come precipitously close to the rocks.

There is a crucial moment when it comes to your awareness that you are drifting and you know you could shift. It's like waking up from a nap on a beautiful day and feeling the pull back into dreamland—do you choose to pry yourself out of bed or sink back into comfortable sleep? Being unconscious can have that same mesmerizing quality, like the mythological Sirens who pulled sailors into the rocks with their sweet and beautiful song. Just being aware of the seductiveness of Reactive Brain and the accompanying drifts that we use to handle our uncomfortable physiology can help us choose to use a Shift Tool—any Shift Tool!—even when we don't want to. Then we can steer our boat just that little bit to where we can once again catch the wind and start sailing free.

For a quick reference of Shift Tools, see Appendix B.

Answers to Exercise 3: Creating Unarguable Statements

1. I'm afraid I'm not lovable.
2. I feel mad because I wanted you to come home sooner, and I didn't get what I want.
3. I'm afraid of taking that route.
4. I feel mad, sad, and scared. I'm having thoughts like "I'm a loser."
5. I notice my body contracting.
6. I feel afraid about not having enough money.
7. I notice I have a story about our sex life. I feel scared and sad; I would like to create more connection with you.
8. I'm afraid people will judge me based on the way I keep house.

Points to Steer By

- To be unconscious is to simply react according to one's conditioning, with no particular ability to choose something different. Becoming conscious of our internal experience opens the door to shifting that experience instead of just drifting along through life.
- Being open to *what is* without criticizing or comparing allows the light touch of awareness to keep you in the zone of being awake without clamping down on yourself, pulling you into contraction.
- Shifting is simply about waking up and becoming aware that you have gone into an old pattern, have started reacting, are on automatic, are drifting.
- Remembering to simply notice your inner world will keep you in your own experience, and being in your own experience means that you are facing into *what is*.

- Attention as an agent of change is the power behind being conscious.
- There are two key ground rules in the land of the unarguable truth:
    - Anyone gets to feel anything anytime for any reason.
    - "Because I want to [or don't want to]" is the best reason there is.
- We get angry for two reasons:
    - Because we don't get what we want (we're thwarted).
    - Because we get what we don't want (we're intruded upon).
- Wondering is the first step to creativity.
- If you can't remember to do anything else, taking a deep breath will get you out of irons and fill your sails.
- To really live is to play. How could you be enjoying yourself more right now?
- Appreciation allows you to jump Above the Line by focusing on the positive; choosing to love your experience will zip you even further up your Inner Map to expanded states that support magic happening in you and around you.
- Drifts take us off course from our bigger intentions in life as we give in to the short-term gratification of moving away from what doesn't feel good while ignoring the long-term consequences of our choices.

5

Charting Your Course

Though pleas'd to see the dolphins play, I mind my compass and my way.
~ Matthew Green

OK, Matey, you've got some aptitude with locating yourself and your relation-ship on your maps. You can get yourself out of irons and find the wind again. Now that you know where you are and how to get moving, where do you want to go, and how do you make sure you get there? The next step to making yourself seaworthy is to master the ultimate tool of navigation: the compass. Compasses are essential in setting your course; they are even more important in helping you stay on track. And it makes sense to use your compass to help you get where you want to go.

The human ability to notice our own state and then consciously choose what we want to create next sets us apart from all other species. Animals follow their instincts to feed themselves and find habitats; humans can fantasize, dream up, imagine, and move toward realities that don't yet exist in physical form. When we are in Reactive Brain, our lives can feel flat as we follow old conditioned patterns, perhaps living lives that are little more than animal-like, as we plod along, going to jobs that allow us to get food and pay the rent or being in relationships that mirror pack-like hierarchy. Charting your own course means shaking out of the robot-like existence of Reactive Brain and letting your Creative Brain guide you to possibility.

Wanting and Being Willing

Here is a big question, one that will open you up to charting your own course: Are you willing to live the life you really want? Answering this question is essential to creating a fulfilling life. It takes you into a new field of potential. Notice that this question is not "Are you living the life you think you should be living?" or "Does your life reflect your highest values?" or even "Are you happy?" Deciding whether you are willing to live the life you *really* want takes you beyond superficial measures into the deeper realms of your heart's true desires.

Let's get clear about the difference between being willing and wanting. We want a lot of things: fancy cars, a big house, a promotion, a million dollars, a perfect partner. Examining the submerged wanting beneath these lists takes you to the true wanting that defines you, that gives you a reflection of who you are at your core. In other words, what we *want* in the material world can give us an idea of what we really want, deep down, if we are *willing* to look.

Let's pick something from the list of wants above and examine the deeper levels. How about a million dollars? Sounds great, doesn't it? Who wouldn't want that? But let's go underneath that want. What would you do right now if someone handed you a million dollars? Would you quit your job? So you could do what? Go off to the woods and write poetry? Maybe spend your life on a sailboat, sailing around the world? Or just stay home with your kids? Do you see that what you really want is to write poetry, sail around the world, be with your kids? Now let's go below that. What is it about poetry, sailing, or being a parent that calls to you? Ah! Maybe what you really want is to express your creativity in an ongoing way, or be at one with nature, or live in continuous connection with your loved ones.

People get very confused about this. We think, "Yes! A million dollars is what I want!" Then we tie our lives up in pursuing the million dollars, working sixty hours a week, making risky investments, or buying lottery tickets. What we don't realize is that we have decided on a solution—that is, the million dollars—before we have figured out the issue in our lives we want to resolve. Understanding what you *really* want, the bottom line wanting of your heart, is the key move to creating the life you want because, of course, your life is simply the compilation of all of the moments of what you have chosen as you go. Then there are the small wants along the way—"I really want to dance to loud, rhythmic music right now"—as well as the most expanded, visionary wants—"I want to be totally fulfilled in what I do" or "I want to live in integrity, discovering joy and magic every day."

Let's split these apart here. Your biggest wants—your vision for your life—are really the points on the horizon you are sailing toward. Living from the moment-to-moment wants allows you to be increasingly aligned with your essential self so that you are fueled by your full power as you steer toward your vision. Before any of this can happen, however, take a big breath and try out this idea: *I choose to live a life in which every moment of every day, I'm doing what I really want to do, and I'm not doing what I don't want to do.*

Many people would see this as the hallmark of selfishness: How could this be possible?! Who would do all of the hard work? Who would change the diapers or sit up with a sick child? Who would dig the ditches, scrub the toilets, or pay the bills? Well, maybe people who want to, people who sat down and asked the question "What do I *really* want to be doing?" and found themselves most drawn to nurturing children, or working with their physical strength, or loving the concrete steps of writing checks and sending them off.

Somewhere we got way off track with doing what we want to do. Suffering through life became the hallmark of being a "good person" so that the more difficult one's life is, the more virtuous. The high rates of depression, anxiety, and addiction in our culture would suggest we are, indeed, a very virtuous people, people whose lives are so out of alignment with our real selves it takes caffeine to keep us going through the day and TV and alcohol or sleeping pills to wind us down at night.

When they hear the question "What do you really want?" many people haven't a clue how to answer it. They have spent their whole lives talking themselves into what they should want—"I should be an accountant so I'll always be able to get a job!" or "I should have kids; my biological clock is ticking!"—until they have tamped down the parts of themselves that have been trying to tell them all along what they really want. They might be able to tell what they don't want—"I hate this commute" or "Thank God I only have to be at this job for seven more years"—but shifting into what they do want can feel like waking up in a different universe.

Are you ready to step into this universe, be one of the first occupants of this brand new world? This is the world where the virtue is in doing what you love. Imagine it: Everyone you encounter—grocery store check-out people, customer service representatives, parents, dentists, kids at school, factory workers—is thrilled with what they are doing. They can't wait to get to work, or to school, or home because what they do is fulfilling, engaging, and downright enjoyable for them. When you talk to them, it is clear that they have taken total responsibility for their lives so that if something is out of alignment, they are taking steps to correct it. Customer service representatives can take real actions to rectify the problem; parents can speak the truth about their needs; school kids can give actual feedback about why they are bored or unhappy. Of course, such a world would not include sixty-hour or even forty-hour workweeks or school days beginning at 7:30 a.m. It would reflect actual human needs for activity, fun, rest, and fulfillment.

Knowing that we are probably a little way from such a world, how about taking some small steps toward having the life you want? It would begin with becoming skilled at finding and using your own built-in compass. Later we will go over how to set your destination point on the horizon and how to use your compass and maps together to continually orient yourself toward where you really want to go.

We all have our own personal inner compass. It is the place in our bodies that "lights up" or expands when we create what we really want. Similarly, it goes dense and contracts when we don't (sounds familiar, doesn't it?).

Exercise 1: *Calibrating Your Internal Compass*

It's time to calibrate your Internal Compass. There are two parts to this exercise:

- Learning how to identify what you really want.
- Finding out what you really *don't* want.

What you really want:

- Think of something you already know you love or feel excited about. It might be an activity, like golf or knitting, or a place, or a certain food, or a beloved person or animal.
- While you think about this something that you love or feel excitement for, breathe and notice your body sensations. What do you notice? Is there any sensation of opening or flow? It might be in your chest or your belly.
- Keep breathing into this feeling and let it get really big so you can recognize it anytime, anywhere.
- Take an inner snapshot of the details of what it feels like. Imagine this being your main draw toward what you want, like a gentle current pulling you along your own personal river.

What you really don't *want:*

- What is something you absolutely cannot stand? Maybe a smell or a talk-show host? Perhaps a kind of music or a color?
- Let your attention move into whatever it is. What is happening in your body now? Do you detect any sense of pulling in or contraction, a kind of flattening out?
- Let that feeling intensify and mark it in your mind. Like drifting out of one's lane on the highway onto the rumble strips, your body will tighten immediately to send you the signal of what you don't want.

Want versus Really Want: Your Internal Compass

Now you have got the two points on your Internal Compass that are your extremes: the body sensations of what you love and the body sensations of what you abhor. You can download a PDF of the Internal Compass at www.JuliaColwell.com.

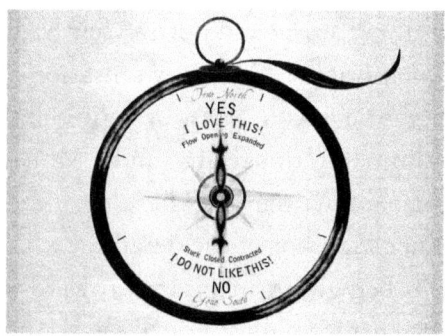

Tuning in to your Internal Compass is a reliable way to gauge what you want to move toward and what you want to move away from. In fact, these two categories—what we like and what we dislike—distinguish two of the most elemental ways that our bodies give us information—if we are willing to tune in to them. Katie Hendricks has labeled these as our "full-body Yes" and "full-body No" to emphasize how, if we listen, our bodies will give us the guidance we need. Responding to our Yes takes us toward what we intuitively want to be doing, who we want to connect with, what we really want. Tuning in to our No allows us to set the boundaries that we really want, keeps us from making bad agreements, and eliminates resentment from our lives.

Fully stepping into what you really want, however, places you face-to-face with two potential stumbling blocks: disappointment and fear. Somewhere along the line many of us figured out that, in order not to experience the helpless anger of disappointment, we could just stop wanting anything at all. Because we didn't know how to move through feelings quickly, the best we could do was shut down our wanting so that we wouldn't have to feel the letdown of not getting what we wanted. While that strategy is understandable, it is short-sighted. Not getting what we really want can feel defeating, but it is really just a temporary setback. The moment of realizing we didn't win the lottery and resigning ourselves to going back to the job we hate could be the signal to stop, breathe, sit back, and wonder: What did we *really* want? Getting the *thing* is always about getting whatever it is we *think* the thing will get us.

Being afraid of disappointment can stop us from wanting; so can the fear of actually moving toward what we want. Perhaps you imagine finding a new job, one that would challenge and fulfill you. As you dream about your new position, you feel that wonderful expansion in your body, your personal "Yes" indicator. Then you talk to a friend who reminds you about the tight job market. Immediately your stomach tightens. You then mistake this for having a "No" about the job, and you stop yourself from moving toward it.

> Amy is a researcher for a major pharmaceutical company but feels bored and unfulfilled. She wants to help people more directly, so she is considering going back to school for a degree in nursing. She just can't seem to take the step

to apply. As she sorts through her past, she remembers longing to be a physician when she was in her early twenties and then focusing on taking care of her ailing mother instead. As she imagines going to medical school now, she bursts into tears in recognition of her true calling. "But I'm too scared—I'm too old to start that now!" Her fear continues to keep her from stepping into what she really wants.

Let's go back to that key question: Are you willing to live the life that you really want?

Is it sounding any more possible?

As we talked about in Chapter 4, the way many of us manage our fear and the potential for disappointment is through drifts—the variety of behaviors we use to stay unconscious and out of contact with our real selves. Choosing to drift can seem like we are doing what we want to do—"I want to watch TV" or "I want to eat that chocolate cake" or "I want a cigarette"—when really these are all methods of keeping ourselves from feeling our bodies. It is possible to be consciously unconscious, but doing so is different from tuning in to what you truly want.

Exercise 2: Finding "Want," "Don't Want," and Drifts

Take a moment to consider how you spend your waking hours through the week. As you scan through the days, consider these questions:

- What percentage of the time are you currently doing what you *want* to do?
- What percentage of the time are you doing things you
- *don't* want to do?
- What percentage of the time are you drifting so you don't have to face into knowing the difference?
- What would it be like to be doing what you want to do 100% of the time?

Want, Need, and Crave

Here are two more things to consider when exploring your wants: the distinction between *want* and *need* and the difference between *wanting* and *craving*. You may have noticed that the word "need" has not been getting any attention here. Humans *need* the basics, such as air, water, food, and shelter. However, when we say we *need* attention or respect, for example, aren't we really putting ourselves in the Victim position? "Needing" attention or "needing" respect has a very different feel from "wanting" attention or "wanting" respect, doesn't it? Choosing to use the word "want" whenever you can adds to your own sense of empowerment.

What about the word "craving"? How can we tell the difference between what we want and what we crave? Wanting is a deep and reliable signal from your gut about what sings to you, what moves you toward aligning with your true self. Craving, on the other hand, is an impulse to tamp down the uncomfortable feelings that arise when we are out of integrity with ourselves. Following a craving to eat ice cream or to gamble is generally a move away from—and a disguise of—our real wants. Our cravings are like the call of the Sirens to smash ourselves on the rocks rather than take the risk to sail out to the open sea of our bigger vision, our biggest selves.

Finding Your Course

Steering from your compass and maps isn't of much use if you don't know where you want to go. What is the course of your most essential self, the one that will allow you to experience your deepest fulfillment?

As you have tuned in to the "wants below your wants"—that is, the bottom line of what you really want—you have been getting some experience in listening to your inner voice. Knowing how to hear and respond to your real self, your soul, your core, or your essence, is to find your own True North. Once you have developed an ongoing relationship with this deepest place in you, you can sail through life, knowing that each day's voyage is a beautiful expression of who you really are. It's truly living life as the journey, not just waiting for the destination.

Tuning In to Your Core Self

As you might imagine, tuning in to your core self is a skill cultivated over time. There are two parts to aligning with your core self: understanding your life purpose—that is, what you are really here to do—and creating ongoing intentions that support doing whatever you are here to do. Your life purpose is the destination point on the horizon, what you are steering toward. Your intentions keep you in the vicinity, helping you stay on course and co-create with the winds of nature. Intentions are the powerful first step toward manifesting what you want. You start with unrealized potential—space; then you have an idea; then you find words to express your idea. Writing down and speaking the words of your intentions begin the process of birthing your idea into the world.

Answering the questions in the exercise below will create some initial connection points between your outer self (your social self who interacts with others) and your deepest aspects (your true, unique self). Don't worry about coming up with answers; instead, let yourself play and try different ideas. As you write, tune in to your Internal Compass to find out where these ideas take you. How good are you willing to feel in your life every day? Between your life purpose and your intentions, you have what you need to sail through your life, enjoying every day. And as you get the hang of this, you will probably notice that as you are steering along from your moment-to-moment wanting, you will naturally be in flow with your intentions and moving toward fulfilling your life purpose.

Exercise 3: Tuning In to Your Core Self

If you like, you can download a PDF version of the questions below from the Duffle Bag at www.JuliaColwell.com.

Part 1: Discovering Your Life Purpose

1. If someone came in right now and aimed a gun at you, demanding to know what your life purpose is, what would you tell them?
2. In the next five minutes, write down everything you can think of that you have always enjoyed or loved to do. Don't think too much—just write.
3. Now consider this: What are those things you love to do? That you lose yourself in? That you can't wait to do? That you'd choose to do over anything else? That you've had fun doing?
4. Circle the top five items on your list, the ones that take you highest up your Internal Compass. Let yourself marinate in the idea of spending the majority of your time doing those things.
5. Imagine that you're lying on your deathbed looking back over your life. Did you accomplish what you wanted to? What was that?
6. OK, it's time to get your ship in the water. Finish this sentence: To be fulfilled, I will live out my life purpose, which is to . . .

Here are some examples of actual life purposes people have imagined:

- I invite dreams.
- My purpose is to love everyone and everything.
- I'm here to help humans create a new and loving relationship with animals.

- (My own): I'm a friendly elevator operator, joining people as they move up and down the ladder of consciousness.

Part 2: Creating Effective Intentions

As you write down your intentions, make sure you verbalize them in the positive: "It is my intention to live in abundance" instead of "It is my intention not to be poor," and write it in the present tense. To help you out, here are six areas that will get you started on listing your intentions:

- Who you are in the world:

    Example: It is my intention that I live in love and appreciation every moment.
    Now you: It is my intention . . .

- Relationships:

    Example: It is my intention that I continually expand into love with my partner.
    Yours: It is my intention . . .

- Health:

    Example: It is my intention that I create perfect health, making choices every day that support my well-being.
    Yours: It is my intention . . .

- Inner World / Spirituality:

    Example: It is my intention that I take time every day to cultivate my relationship with my inner self.

Yours: It is my intention . . .

- Career:

    Example: It is my intention that I create a meaningful and fulfilling career path.
    Yours: It is my intention . . .

- Money:

    Example: I live in an ongoing flow of abundance. Yours: It is my intention . . .

Keep your intentions list handy and speak them out loud every day.

Combining Charts

Now that you are getting better at charting your own course, let's make it more complex. Let's add in another person who also is charting her or his course—a partner! Uh-oh. You have been working on getting everything you want and seeing how to make that happen. Can both people get everything they want? How can two individuals steer together through life toward their biggest visions as well as from their Internal Compasses for each moment?

Answering these questions is crucial; if they are left unanswered, the initial bliss of relationship becomes power struggle and burden. People lapse into fighting over the helm, or they resign themselves to taking turns deciding who gets to go where, believing that co-creating a course is a mysterious ideal, available to only a few lucky couples who come from very collaborative backgrounds or who simply stumble around until they figure it out. Most people are confused about what they want, and it becomes even more difficult to figure out what we want when we get into relationships. There is a prevailing notion that it is better to be "unselfish" and willing to compromise than to know—or to speak—what we want in the first place. You might recognize this in the wet blanket tossing game:

> *Partner 1: What do you want to do?*
> *Partner 2: I don't know. What do you want to do?*
> *Partner 1: Whatever you want to, Dear!*
> *Partner 2: No, really, I don't care!*

In our attempt to be a "good partner," we often go blurry and give up what we want. While this selflessness can feel noble and act as a momentary conflict buffer, it generally leads to increasing resentment and a contraction of self that ultimately rebounds into much bigger problems. People who think they are being gallant by "not caring" about decisions take on an undefined quality. Since our essential self is made known to others by our unique responses to life—how we feel, what we like, what we don't like—dropping these responses keeps us unknown and unpredictable. And since our real self has to show up sooner or later, others have a sense of waiting for the other shoe to drop—which it will eventually, though people try to ward off this inevitability with the declaration, "I need space!" and go away from their partner to do what they really wanted to do all along.

We cannot keep our true self hidden forever, not without the help of a deadening agent like an addiction. Even then, the true self leaks out in secretive behaviors like having affairs, overeating, using drugs and abusing alcohol, spending money, viewing Internet porn, gambling. Or we take on passive aggressive behaviors like being late, forgetting, or breaking agreements. *Self must be expressed.*

This willingness to not speak what one really wants creates most of the other reasons behind the failure of relationships. You have heard and seen them all; maybe you have spoken or experienced them yourself. "I need to find myself," a wife says after years of catering to her children and husband. "Life is too short," says the man whose clandestine romance with his office colleague results in divorce. Affairs and drug use and credit-card debts finally come to light, and the partner is flabbergasted, feels betrayed. Broken agreements turn into accusations of irresponsibility and judgments about maturity. Addictions become long-standing and debilitating. Deadening oneself leads to the familiar refrain "I love you; I'm just not *in* love with you." The short-sightedness of compromise can be seen in the common backlash that occurs after endings of relationships: "Now I can do all those things I stopped doing when I got married." The implied message, of course, is that we blame our partner for our choices to not say what we really wanted.

Here is the alternative to this dismal landscape. Ask this ongoing, creative question: How can we both get *everything* we want?

When we are in Reactive Brain, this is a nearly impossible question to answer. Reactive Brain is about survival; survival is about contraction. From that place on the Inner Map, what we see is scarcity, which necessarily implies competition. Our survival-oriented brain tells us there is not enough to go around, and suddenly we're fighting with our partner for scraps. Under these circumstances, people tighten down and see few possibilities. Bargaining and scorekeeping become part of this landscape. Here is what this contracted behavior looks like:

> *Partner 1: I'd like to get new furniture for the living room.*
> *Partner 2: We can't afford it.*
> *Partner 1: Sure we can!*
> *Partner 2: Yeah, right, if I work more.*
> *Partner 1: Or you could stop spending so much going out to the bar with your friends.*
> *Partner 2: That's the only fun I have. Why don't you quit going shopping?*
> *Partner 1: The kids have to have new clothes. Plus, you're never around. What else am I going to do?!*

Can you feel the passion-kill of this exchange? Is there anything familiar about it?

The expanded state of "There is plenty of room for us both to get everything we want" is the hallmark of the honeymoon phase. Each person feels loved and valued and can relax into the connection. To preserve this wondrous time, people try to be generous with the deferential "Whatever you want, Honey." Inevitably, however, Reactive Brain gets triggered, and what was a sweet offering can take on the tone of resignation or seething annoyance. This contraction into "There isn't enough to go around, so I have to fight for what I want or give in" is really what ends the honeymoon.

The key to each person getting what he or she wants is to make agreements from Creative Brain. This is where the Relationship Map is extremely useful to navigate by. Making great and enlivening agreements becomes a combination of staying Above the Line—or recognizing that you have dipped Below the Line and stopping the conversation to create a shift—and using the Internal Compass of what each person really wants until you create a new possibility together. Here is how Partners 1 and 2 would sound, using this method of staying on course:

Partner 1: I'd like to get some new furniture for the living room.

Partner 2: Hmm. Will you tell me more about what it is you want about that?

Partner 1: Well, when I walk into our home, it doesn't feel as inviting as I'd like.

Partner 2: Yeah, I've noticed that. And I feel some fear about money. Now that we're talking about this, I notice I'm working more hours than I want to be.

Partner 1: Yes, I miss you!

Partner 2: I miss you, too. I think I've let myself get caught up in this cycle of worrying about money and then trying to solve it by working more.

Partner 1: I'm wondering if you're getting what you want.

Partner 2: I do love my job. I guess what's true is that I just haven't made our relationship a priority. Then I feel lonely, so I get all caught up in my work.

Partner 1: Aww (embracing Partner 2). OK, how do we both get what we want? Hmm. What I really want is to make the living room more inviting. I could do some cool things with paint—I've got some interesting ideas.

Partner 2: Yeah, and we could move the furniture, see how it would look. I'll help. What I want is to spend more time with you anyway. Maybe we could fool around while we try the sofa in a new place . . .

This feels a lot different, doesn't it? When we're living from Creative Brain, new possibilities emerge. Two people together interacting from their Creative Brains allows for an interaction that is like gently tossing an idea back and forth in a way that feels playful and joyful because each can play off of the other. Ultimately, then, partnership is a place where each person can express his or her essential self. Then a third entity, the relationship, is created from the blending of each self in every interaction.

Do you want to create a relationship that is a wonderful combination of two essential selves? If you do, answer these three key questions:

- Is it all right with you if you get everything you want?
- Is it all right with you if your partner gets everything he or she wants?
- Are you willing for both of you to get everything you both want all the time?

This really is possible. And creating such a partnership rests on the skill you were practicing earlier in the chapter, considering what you *think* you want—like a million dollars—and figuring out what you *really* want. When you both do that, even the most seemingly polar opposite wants can find common ground.

For example, one person wants the house to be orderly, and the other, who keeps "trying" but invariably leaves her stuff around in piles, wants—well, with some questioning, wants to feel relaxed, not worried about what is where. We'll call them John and Veronica, knowing they are stand-ins for couples everywhere.

John: I like things picked up and put where they belong. I don't like everything spread around where I can trip over it. Plus I lose things. Hmm—what I want about this is to know where my stuff is, how to find it easily. OK, that's not really the bottom line—what I want is to move through life with ease. I get in a hurry, then can't find my keys—I want to slow down, be more present. Having stuff all put away has been a way for me to deal with how hurried I really am. I guess I hurry out the door to not miss Veronica. If I go fast, I don't have to feel sad. I want to feel what I'm really feeling and tell her about it.

Veronica: I don't like to spend time dealing with stuff. I'd rather be doing whatever I want. Yeah, I want to do whatever I want. Well, is that the bottom line? As I'm saying this, I feel kind of foggy. I see how I stay foggy, and having my belongings everywhere really is a sign of how much I'm not in my body. Yeah, and it's a way to stay one step away from John, to not be connected with him. It's like my things are a buffer between me and him. So what do I want—I want to be present and tell him how afraid I am to be really connected. When we go there, are right there with each other, it just blows my socks off—I want to get better and better at staying present, really being with him.

We thought John wanted stuff to be put away; he really wants to feel what he is feeling and tell Veronica. Veronica said she didn't care about order, but with some musing a different issue surfaced about connecting with John and with herself. So what about the issue of putting stuff away? Typically when couples get to the real issues, what seemed to be a problem no longer has the charge it once carried. When the unconscious factors have been unearthed, deadlocks dissipate and each person tends to become interested in participating in a new way. Veronica's new desire to be present could result in extra attention to her surroundings; John's willingness to feel what he is really feeling could move him out of his focus on what is wrong around him and into an ability to fully relax and enjoy himself, no matter what objects are where.

Let's reorient and apply your skills with your Inner Map, Relationship Map, and Internal Compass to steer through what can be choppy waters. The path toward figuring out how to get what we want in a partnership can easily trigger us into Reactive Brain so that we behave like animals competing for scarce resources. Moving back into Creative Brain allows us to access a much larger field of possibilities, where there is plenty of room for each person to get what he or she really wants, once each has taken the crucial step of figuring out what that is.

Exercise 4: Everybody Gets What They Want

Get out your Inner Map and Relationship Map as well as your Internal Compass, and do this exercise with your partner. Notice if you start to drift Below the Line into Reactive Brain; if you do, stop and use one of your Shift Tools from Chapter 4.

When you've returned to Creative Brain, continue this process.

1. Take a moment to breathe and remind yourselves that the goal is to come up with a really creative solution that reflects the best of both of you.
    a. Person 1: State what you want.
    b. Person 2: Ask, "Is that the bottom line of what you really want?"
    c. Person 1: Reflect on this and restate what you want.
    d. Continue until you both have the sense that Person 1 really has reached the bottom line, her real want that is under the surface want.
2. Switch roles and repeat substeps a–d.
3. Brainstorm creative solutions with the question "How can we both get *everything* we want?" Push yourselves to come up with some ideas that might seem crazy or off-the-wall.
4. Now come back to the solution that feels the best to both of you. As you try it on, can you breathe? Does your body feel expansive?

5. Check this solution: Does it feel good enough to both of you that it is easy and fun to actually do? If so, agree to the solution and *write it down*. If not, go back to step 3 and continue until you agree.

Exercise 5: Creating Your Vision Together

This exercise is about co-creating from each of your most expanded Creative Brains. You'll need something to write on, something to write with, some magazines if you'd like to work with images, and something soft and light to toss back and forth, like a hacky-sack or balloon.

1. Start tossing[32] the object back and forth, starting with this phrase: *What I most want in a relationship is . . .*
2. Toss back and forth, letting each person build on the last toss. It could sound like this:

    Person 1: What I most want in a relationship is—hot sex.
    Person 2: What I most want in a relationship is—hot sex that feels really connected and intimate.
    Person 1: What I most want in a relationship is hot sex that feels connected and intimate, and I want a lot of fun.
    Person 2: What I most want is a lot of fun that feels safe, but right on the cusp so we're both challenged.
    Person 1: Yeah, I want to be challenged and have adventures that take us out of the everyday.

3. Keep going until you each feel heard, and everything you can think of has been said.
4. Now sit down and write key words and phrases.
5. After you've written them all down (or cut and pasted them from the magazines), sit back and make sure you've got everything that you both really want.

Points to Steer By

- The human ability to notice our own state and then consciously choose what we want to create next sets us apart from all other species.
- Deciding whether you are willing to live the life you *really* want takes you beyond the superficial into the deeper realms of your heart and soul's true desires.
- This is a world where the virtue is in doing what you love.
- Our own personal inner compass is the place in our body that "lights up" or expands when we're around (or considering) what we want—and becomes dense and contracts when we're around (or considering) what we don't want.
- Getting the *thing* is always about getting whatever it is we think the thing will get us.
- Allowing yourself to act from your full-body Yes and full-body No means you are steering your own course, no matter what direction the winds blow.
- Intentions are the powerful first step toward manifesting what you want.
- Self must be expressed. If it is not expressed directly, it will leak through indirectly.
- Ask this ongoing, creative question: How can we both get *everything* we want?
- Making great and enlivening agreements is a combination of staying Above the Line and using the Internal Compass of what each person really wants until you create a new possibility together.

6

Drain the Bilge!

The cure for anything is salt water—sweat, tears, or the sea.
                                                    ~Isak Dinesen

Are you starting to smell the salt air, having visions of sailing across the open sea? Well, Sailor, there are a couple more crucial skills to get under your cap before heading out into the ocean blue. In this chapter you will learn how to drain the bilge—that is, move the old emotional energy out of your body, energy that weighs you down—so that you can really get moving. Not being willing to fully feel emotions all the way through is like being an old ship trying to make headway while continuously taking on water. Understanding how to drain dense emotional energy from your body is key to staying in the continuous sensation of flowing through your life and not running aground. Before starting to drain that energy, however, it is helpful to understand more about how emotions work.

The Role of Emotions

Emotions are an elegantly crafted system tying together one's inner and outer worlds. The intricate physiology of emotions allows each of us to have our unique template of response to whatever is going on around us. The fear that gets us to run out of a burning building, the grief of losing a loved one, the joy of holding a new baby, or the anger of being unable to get what we want each carries important information about what our worlds mean to us. Taking the time to pull apart the more intricate emotions—like shame, disappointment, or pride—can tell us where we are in our own network of social hierarchy. Our emotions are like a database of rich information that sends signals from our bodies to our minds. To be able to tune in to and interpret those signals is to be able to read our own weather and use that information to figure out what actions we want to take.

This is a good time to get out your Inner Map. Let's look at some of the most primal emotions, the ones that have been programmed into mammalian brains for millennia: Sadness, Fear, and Anger. Each has a different level of density and triggers varying places in the body. Try this: Remember a time when you felt sad. Does your chest feel heavy? Do you feel a lump in your throat? Now remember a time you felt afraid. Maybe your pulse quickens or you feel a flutter in your stomach. How about a memory of being angry? Does your fist or jaw clench or your neck tighten? All of these physiological responses are preparing you to move through the experience of the loss of something or someone important to you, or to get away fast, or to defend yourself. When you let yourself tune in to these sensations, you will have crucial information about how your unique self processes information coming through your body about the external world.

Having built-in signals for sadness, fear, and anger are essential to mammalian survival. Sadness is a response to the loss of those we've attached ourselves to. (Access to attachment figures is more important than food for the survival of a baby mammal, so even adults experience chaotic physiological symptoms when cut off from significant loved ones.) Fear may signal us to flee from danger, and anger may signal us to confront danger. Sadness, fear, and anger are the pathways that run directly from experience to reaction. Reactive Brain is vital to survival, so it is easily provoked.

While vitally important, however, sadness, fear, and anger don't provide a wide enough range of information to the evolving mammal. For those animals that gather in packs, social hierarchy and separation of roles add a level of complexity to pack functioning that makes the pack more adept at finding food and habitat. As you look at the other states on the Inner Map, you can see how the mammalian brain created a way to immediately recognize status: the proud leader could humiliate the weaker-ranked animal through the aggression of anger, creating responses of fear and the ultimate collapse into the submissive postures denoted by despair, guilt, and shame.[33]

All of the responses that are Below the Line are about staying alive. You can recognize them by the hallmarks of being in Reactive Brain: physiological mobilization or immobilization (those qualities that your Pressure Gauge helps you to detect). While people tend to have a lot of judgment about others or themselves being in Reactive Brain, the brain itself doesn't care; it is doing its job, which is to ensure survival.

Those chemicals that support the quick reaction, however, leave a trail behind them. Hormones that are emitted in response to threat—such as adrenalin, cortisol, and others—all need to be metabolized, processed through the body. Tense muscles need to be relaxed, heart rate and breathing regulated. Thus, the primary mechanism for processing emotion is to actually *feel* it, to be in direct experience of the actual sensations that our bodies use to communicate our emotional state to us. Putting our attention on the emotional sensations acts to break down and absorb the energy of the emotion, something like a digestive process. (In fact, in Ayurvedic practice, one cause of disease is "undigested emotion.") However, humans have the capacity to shut down this process. When we feel overwhelmed by sadness, fear, anger, or any other emotional experience, nearly all of us have developed techniques to simply shut ourselves off from our experience of the emotions, which pushes them under the surface.

Draining the bilge, then, is about moving undigested dense emotions out of the body. These could be from a current situation that triggers Reactive Brain, such as when we perceive an actual threat (like being in a skidding car or watching someone's fist draw back to hit us). However, whenever a present-day circumstance activates a reaction that seems out of proportion to what is going on, it is *always* triggering feelings from the past that have not yet been processed.

This is an important point, one to be stressed. When we feel awash in a reactive response, we want to believe ourselves. Of course we're angry with the guy who cut us off in traffic—who wouldn't be! Well, a large percentage of the population, actually. When we take the time to give our attention to what is really happening in our bodies, we can invariably find the trail back to the original situation where we withdrew our attention, shut ourselves off from the emotion, and as a result, never processed it.

> *Maggie and Pat bickered and fought over every little thing. "I just want to be heard and seen!" Pat insisted. As we traced back through her sensations of anger, she remembered fighting with her mother, who would ultimately cut off the conflict by sending her to her room.*
>
> *Tom was tired of always being the one to initiate sex, so he stopped bringing it up. He felt resentful and unappreciated—wasn't physical intimacy what marriage was supposed to be about?! As he breathed into his body and placed his full attention on his experience, he noticed tightness in his chest and throat—not anger at all, but sadness. As he stayed with the sadness, he had a memory of wanting to play with his older brother, who didn't want anything to do with him.*

The process of placing our attention on the actual body sensations of an emotion and staying with them until the real issue emerges is failsafe. These sensations are a reasonable, though exaggerated, response that creates a trail back to the original triggering event. Let's go back to the driver who pulled in front of you. If you took the time to actually pay attention to your body sensations, you might start wondering why you're so angry. You might ask yourself how this response is familiar and follow the thread back in time. Maybe memories of competition with a sibling will surface, or you'll connect with times that you've had a sense of being thwarted by obstacles. In other words, it's not that there is some objective reality of "that guy is a bad driver who deserves my anger." Instead, the body sensations can bring your attention to this question: "What is this big sensation in my body reminding me of from my own past?"

If you get activated in a way that doesn't make sense to you, it doesn't mean you're crazy; it just means that there are old issues you need to resolve. In fact, this is one of the gifts of intimacy: being close to someone creates countless opportunities to trigger old unprocessed emotion. Unfortunately, most couples aren't so excited about this, instead viewing this activation as an indication of deep-seated problems, either in the relationship or with one of the people in the couple. So they put their effort into not getting triggered, giving each other detailed instructions—The List of What You Need to Do So That I Feel Happy—about what the partner should do to keep this triggering from occurring. ("Smile at me when I come in the door." "Don't drink—you remind me of my alcoholic father." "Won't you PULLEAZE pick up after yourself?! Clutter makes me insane!") It is inevitable that neither person will remember these detailed lists when Reactive Brain takes over, though often this is used as further evidence of problems. ("You said you wouldn't drink! You lied to me! How can I trust you?!) Now each can add this lack of follow-through to their sense of failure as a couple.

Another outcome of not understanding how the present triggers the past is that a couple will begin to avoid those activities that have the potential to activate one or both of them. Sex is an area rife with this sort of avoidance. The deep emotional connection of making love often brings old feelings to the surface, which can surprise people if they believe sex should just be fun and happy. Sobbing from old sadness or freezing with terrifying memories is not what most people expect from being sexual. Without any way to handle this emotional upwelling, couples sometimes back away from whatever might bring on these deep feelings.

Staying in connection with your partner, then, is a matter of letting yourself have your emotional experience, no matter what, and then being willing to follow wherever it takes you until you are done with it. Likewise, if it is your partner who is having emotions, your task is to stay connected by leaving space for him to have his feelings *without taking those feelings personally*. As you become more adept at separating out whose feelings are whose, it will become increasingly clear that emotions are only about the person having them and have *nothing* to do with the other person. This means the partner who has done or said the "wrong thing"—whatever triggered the other's emotional response—is not responsible for the response. The response was lying in wait in the responder's body, like gasoline ready to be sparked.

Life is about becoming a good wave-rider: expecting that there will be small waves of emotion that are from typical, day-to-day existence, and then the really big breakers that are messages from the past. The waves from the past can feel like they are about to pull you over the brink or capsize your ship. And they are also the waves that can really sweep you along, washing out old, long-standing issues—if you and your partner are willing to ride them.

Riding the waves of emotion is a lot easier when you know what to expect. Here are some tips:

- Emotion is energy—*energy in motion*. Emotion gets activated to get our attention. That's what the tension, tightness, butterflies, lump-in-the-throat, aching, quivering, shaking, contracting is for.
- When we notice the body sensation and place our attention fully on it—in short, when we *hear* the message—the emotion has done its job, so it can dissipate.
- When we don't hear the message, when we divert our attention—by eating, drinking, smoking, self-medicating, or play-

ing computer games, for example—the energy does not dissipate. Unprocessed, the emotional energy lodges in the body, waiting to be triggered.

The trick of riding the waves, then, is to place your full attention on the sensations, the actual energy of the emotion, until you hear the message the sensations were designed to deliver. Your willingness to fully experience your body sensations will dissipate the emotions and allow you to traverse the channel from Below the Line to Above the Line, from Reactive to Creative Brain. Very simple, isn't it? And yet people will drink or smoke themselves to death just so they don't have to feel their emotions. Most of us have the idea that if we focus on these body sensations, our emotions will get bigger and bigger, to the point that we'll explode or become non-functional or go crazy.

What most of us don't know is that the lifespan of most emotions is about two minutes—if we can keep our thoughts out of the experience.[34] There is a very predictable energetic cycle that will happen if we can simply focus on our body sensations. Noticing and breathing into the sensations will first intensify them before it supports them in diffusing out of the body (which is usually when we try to turn them off, believing they'll just get worse and worse). If we stay with the cycle and let the sensations keep building, they will actually reach a crescendo of intensity before diffusing out of the body. This very simple process can seem miraculous to people who have spent their lives avoiding the sensation of emotions.

On the other hand, telling ourselves a story will evoke the emotions over and over, making it impossible to move them at all. When we can't get out of this pattern—feel-think-evoke—we turn to drugs, alcohol, medications, or other addictions to make the feelings go away. If we were willing to experience the pure emotion for the few minutes it lasts, often this self-medicating would be unnecessary.

Most of us don't know that we have a choice: we can re-evoke the emotion and keep running the same stories in our heads, or we can choose to diffuse the energy and feel better in less time than it takes to find the bottle of Valium. Here is how each of these choices might sound in your head:

Re-evoke the emotion:

I feel so scared! Oh no, I hate it when I feel this way! I feel sick to my stomach, I think I might pass out! I better not leave the house. It's a scary, scary world out there. And it's getting worse! Look at the papers—violence, climate change, the world is going downhill fast. And my life is getting worse and worse—I don't think my partner even likes me anymore! Neither do my co-workers. I think my boss is getting ready to fire me. It doesn't matter how hard I try, why do I even try?!

Diffuse the energy:

I notice my stomach is in a knot and I feel jittery; I feel scared! I'm breathing into my stomach, watching the energy get bigger; the knot feels worse, and I feel nauseated now. Energy is bubbling up through my solar plexus. OK, breathing into it, letting myself feel as scared as I feel. My whole abdomen feels filled with energy now; it feels like it could explode. Now I feel really hot. Now I notice my stomach relaxing, the nausea has passed. I can breathe more deeply.

The second person is going to feel a lot better in a matter of minutes. The first one could keep this mental dialogue going for hours, days, maybe even her whole life. And without giving her body any attention, it's likely she'll want to numb out the sensations accompanying her fear with some sort of substance, like alcohol or sugar, anything to make the tension in her body diminish.

It can take a lot of practice to not let ourselves be consumed by our thoughts; meditation and other disciplines are designed to do exactly that. And the more effective we are at getting our minds out of the way of what our bodies can do naturally, the more agile we will be at moving the energy.

Giving ourselves and our emotions full attention in regular doses through the day is key to having a whole relationship with ourselves, as well as to creating deep intimacy with others.

Intimacy is a dynamic loop between two people, where both people can connect to their own internal experiences of whatever their body sensations and emotions are trying to tell them. They can then emerge and communicate to the other about what is going on in that inner world. Then there can be a rhythmic tossing back and forth of each person's experience of what is happening in response to the other's experience. Most of us have no idea that this step is vital to our staying connected with ourselves and with our loved ones, leaving us truly attention deficit.

Draining Emotional Bilge

This process is designed to help you move out the Below-the-Line negative emotions, those that use up our energy if we don't feel them all the way through. To make it easy on yourself, focus on processing the primary emotions of anger, fear, and sadness. For the Above-the-Line emotions, the true challenge is to let them continue to expand without interruption.

As you read through this process, try to apply it to a time (maybe now!) when you felt anger, fear, or sadness. The process is made up of five steps:

1. Locate your state on the Inner Map.
2. Notice and identify your body sensations.
3. Feel and ride the waves of your emotions.
4. Express what is true.
5. Rest.

Ready to do some bilge draining? First let's go through the process in detail; then you'll practice each step in the exercise at the end of the chapter.

Locate your state on the Inner Map.

Notice that when you have bilge to drain, you are always in a state Below the Line. Checking your Inner Map will help you locate exactly where you are—in Anger? Fear? Sadness?—so that you know what kind of energy you want to drain. Now ask yourself: *Is this an issue that is threatening my survival?* If so, let yourself respond accordingly. This is what your body is built for. Maybe you really do need to fight off the mountain lion or run away from the burglar. Be careful about this step, however. Remember in Chapter 2, where you learned how your emotional state creates your thoughts, how you perceive and then influence your current reality? Our mind easily makes up a story about how our partner, our boss, the political opponent really *is* a danger to us. So just because you had an argument with your partner and you're agitated does not mean there is an actual threat. Instead, it is highly likely that old emotional bilge has been brought to the surface.

Notice and identify your body sensations.

What sensations are in your body? Where are they located? Generally, the emotions that really get stuck in us are those that occurred during a time when we perceived a threat and didn't know how to process the resulting emotions. Our bodies were giving us the emotional alarm signals, and we didn't know how to process the emotions after the danger was over, so they somehow got stuck in our bodies.

When activated, emotions show up in our bodies in certain places. For example, fear hangs around in the stomach and solar plexus: your sensations might feel queasy, knotted, or fluttery. Sadness is up in the chest and throat, usually feeling quite heavy, achy, painful, or like a lump. Anger is in those areas that we use to fight: the fists that clench, the shoulders, neck, and jaw that tighten, the lower back that is holding back a kick. It feels hot, tight, compressed, clenched. In general, sticking with this short, simple list of these contracted emotional states—Scared, Sad, Mad—can help you label them even when you are upset.

The trick to knowing what you are really feeling is to get your mind out of the way. It will want to criticize and discard what your body is telling you. That is why it is important to begin by paying attention to your body sensations and finding the emotional response even before you name the emotion. It's easy to think we're angry when we're really frightened, or sad when we're actually angry. Starting with the location of the body sensation will steer you around this obstacle of thinking you know what's true before you've given yourself your full attention.

Noticing sensations and naming emotions are powerful first steps in helping them move through; remember, the point of having emotions is to get our attention. When we start paying attention, the emotions have done their job. Interpreting their meaning is the tricky part: are they from the present or the past? If you can just keep your mind from jumping in (it really wants to be right!), your body really will tell you if the feelings are from the past. You can ask this a couple of ways. You can tune in to your body and see if the feelings feel familiar, especially from your past, particularly from your childhood. You can also just ask your body, "How old do I feel?" Whatever comes to your mind first will be surprisingly accurate to the age you were when the initial—and unprocessed—incident occurred.

Feel your emotions! Ride the waves!

This step is probably the most important one of all, the one that people seem to want to avoid at all costs. We might willingly *say* what we're feeling, but actually *feel* what we're feeling? That takes true courage, the moment of steering out of the familiarity of not feeling your feelings and instead turning fully into what is really going on in your body. This is the moment when you move fully in and on the wave, riding it through whatever form it chooses to take. As the emotion becomes less compressed, your energy will rise, and you might feel like you're surfing. Remember that this part will usually take just a few minutes—if you're willing to fully experience the ride and not let your mind make up stories about how the ride is too scary to stay on.

Get ready to follow the little ripple, the small surge, the billowing swell, or the heaving waves as they sweep you forward, forward, forward. So long as you keep breathing, you won't drown in the briny deep. This is an exciting, sometimes frightening ride: where you previously had some semblance of control by compressing the energy of the emotion, you now are allowing yourself to have the wild, irrepressible experience of letting your body do what it is designed to do: move energy.

Express what is true.

Let your whole body participate in whatever is coming up for you, matching your experience with sound, movements, words, drawings, whatever you'd like. Your own truth has been submerged within this old energy, perhaps for a very long time. As it surfaces, it will tell you exactly and unarguably what was most important about that past experience. Finally, the energy—your truth—gets to be expressed—that is, pressed out of your body.

A key point about expressing emotion is this: You are in control of how to express your emotions. You are not in control of having feelings; that's a natural process that comes and goes like waves on the sand. But how you express them is up to you. This is particularly important in the areas of anger and sexuality, both big energies that tend to cause people trouble. Allowing your anger to surge up through your body is one step; deciding how to express it is an entirely separate issue. Similarly, letting yourself feel your full sexual feelings, no matter when they happen or whom you're with means letting yourself have the richness of your full body experience. Deciding with whom you want to express those feelings gives you choice and allows you to stay in integrity with your agreements with your partner.

Notice that expressing the energy of your truth—verbally or otherwise—releases contracted energy that was clogging you up. Here's where it is important to remember that our emotional energy has *nothing to do with* the other person, or people, or whatever the trigger was. This can be very confusing. It sure looks like it's their fault. You were feeling fine before, and now, since they said/did/didn't do that thing, you're feeling this emotion.

Let's say you get angry with your partner for being late. You feel the surge of mobilizing chemicals—your fists are clenched, you feel pain in your neck—all the signs of anger. As you ride the wave of this anger, noticing it, fully being with it, watching it rise and get big and then dissipate, you could choose to growl or yell or stamp your feet to move the energy. As you experience all of this, remember that your anger has nothing to do with your partner. Your feelings are yours; it's your body. Someone else might have no reaction at all or might feel sad ("He doesn't care about me!") or scared ("I hope she's not hurt!") or happy ("Phew! Dinner wasn't ready yet."). Your reaction comes from *your* experience, *your* thoughts, from *who you are*.

This is a key point in being able to ride out feelings with someone else present. We can get all tangled up in each other's emotions if we don't understand this. If you think you cause your partner's feelings, or vice versa, your attention must go to trying to keep him or her from having a reaction, and that brings you back to The List of What You Need to Do So That I Feel Happy, which, as we've established, is impossible to remember while in Reactive Brain. To keep from getting tangled up, each person must give the other space to have a full feeling cycle without getting in the way *at all*. As you can tell, riding a wave of emotion can take a person's full attention. The best action the other person can take is to simply witness what is happening for the other person, be present for it, and not get in the way by taking it personally.

Let's compare the tangled up version with the one that allows full experience and expression of emotion:

- Emotional Entanglement:

    Partner 1: *I feel so MAD at you! Why are you so LATE?!!*
    Partner 2: *What do YOU have to be mad about? So what I'm ten minutes late. You are so UPTIGHT. Will you please relax and let me have a LIFE?!*
    Partner 1: *How can I relax when I can't even trust you to be on time!*
    Partner 2: *Well, excuuuuuse me, Mr. Perfect. As if you don't ever make a mistake. Like the one from the bank account—$158! Now that was a doozie!*
    Partner 1: *Oh, right, change the subject! I thought we said that issue was over. I can't believe you're bringing it up again. You know, I really hate our relationship.*
    Partner 2: *Yeah, well, you think I like it?!*

- Full Experience/Expression:

    Partner 1: *I feel so MAD at you! You're LATE!* Partner 2: *Hmmm, yes I am. I see you're mad.*
    Partner 1: *Yeah, my fist is clenched, and my jaw is really tight.*
    Partner 2: *I see that. [Breathing.]*
    Partner 1: *I want to move the energy. [Gets up and jumps up and down.] I notice my thoughts are all about how I hate not getting what I want. [Makes a rumbling sound, moving his jaw around.]*
    Partner 2: *Yeah, that makes sense to me.*

Using this approach, partners can be allies, assisting each other in moving energy, whether that energy is from old experiences that have been reactivated or from whatever is currently triggering them into Reactive Brain. Rather than take the other person's emotional reaction personally, we can simply witness it and support the other as she surfs the waves, whether they are tiny ripples or gigantic swells. As each person is able to fully experience her or his own emotions, energy can get unstuck, essence is revealed, and connection and intimacy can return and be heightened.

Rest.

After a big ride through the swells of emotion, be sure to give yourself some downtime to breathe, relax, and celebrate yourself for taking the challenge of having a full self.

Appreciating the Ride

As you are on this fascinating ride, alone or with your partner, remember that every wave has a beginning, a middle, and an end. Sometimes storms come through, whipping up the surf, but they are temporary and will move through. When you stay with the energy of each wave until it crests, you can enjoy the pleasure of riding through its dissipation. Allowing these waves to become an ongoing part of your life and your partnership will keep energy moving and allow you to have the best payoff of all: an alive and passionate relationship.

Exercise 1: Draining Emotional Bilge

You can do this exercise to process current emotions as well as the old bilge that has backed up, weighing you down.

1. Locate yourself on the Inner Map.
    - Are you Above the Line or Below the Line?
    - If you're Below the Line, is there a current threat to

your survival? If so, do something! RUN! FIGHT! FREEZE! If not, continue this process.
- Notice that your body is in Reactive Brain, even though there is no current danger to you.
- Don't believe anything you're thinking.
- Celebrate this opportunity to move out old, unprocessed emotion.

2. Notice your sensations.
    - Where are they in your body?
    - What do your sensations feel like? (Tight, knotted, fluttery, queasy, or something else?)
    - Are you feeling mad, sad, or scared?
    - Are these sensations familiar from childhood?
    - How old do you feel?
    - What does this remind you of?

3. Ride the waves!
    - Breathe into the sensations, letting them get as big as they are.
    - Keep your attention on the sensations themselves, bringing your attention back when your mind wants to divert you with thoughts.
    - Keep going through the waves' peaking, until the sensations dissipate.

4. Express what is true.
    - Match the sensations with any expression you want: making sounds, moving, drawing, writing about what is unarguable, even sculpting in the air.
    - Now that you know what is really going on, is there someone you'd like to tell about your experience?

5. Rest.
    - Appreciate your courage for heading straight into your own storm.
    - Notice what your body feels like without that layer

of old energy stuck in it. Feel the flow that has always existed underneath the density of that bilge.

Points to Steer By

- Emotions are an elegantly crafted system tying together one's inner and outer worlds.
- The primary mechanism for processing emotion is to actually *feel* it, to be in direct experience of the particular sensations that our bodies use to communicate our emotional state to us.
- Whenever a present-day circumstance activates a reaction that seems out of kilter with what is going on, it is *always* triggering feelings from the past that have not yet been processed.
- Being close to someone creates countless opportunities to trigger old unprocessed emotion.
- Your willingness to fully experience your body sensations will dissipate emotions and allow you to traverse the channel from Below the Line to Above the Line, from Reactive to Creative Brain.
- Intimacy is a dynamic loop between two people, where both people can connect with their own internal experiences of whatever their body sensations and emotions are trying to tell them. They can then emerge and communicate to the other what is going on in that inner world.
- The skill to knowing what you are really feeling is to get your mind out of the way.
- Expressing the energy of your truth—verbally or otherwise—releases contracted energy that was clogging you up.
- Our emotional energy has *nothing to do* with the other person, or people, or whatever the trigger was.
- Partners can be allies, assisting each other in moving energy, whether that energy is from old experiences that have been

reactivated or from whatever is currently triggering them into Reactive Brain.

7

Running a Tight Ship

A wet sheet and a flowing sea, / A wind that follows fast / And fills the white and rustling sail / And bends the gallant mast.
~ Allan Cunningham

Imagine the exhilaration of sailing a boat with your partner. You have a good wind behind you; the water is streaming from your prow as it slices through the waves. Your partner has the tiller; the pressure of the rudder in the water pulls and pushes against his or her grip. You're holding the sheet—the rope that winds through the boom and mast—connecting you to the sail. As you pull the sheet in tighter, you feel the rush of speed as the wind tilts the boat precipitously close to the water—maybe you'll capsize! Then you let the sheet out, righting the boat but slowing it down. You feel the rush of co-creating an unbridled ride with the two of you, your boat, the sail, the water, and the wind.

Now try a different image. Even though the wind is readily available, it blows fruitlessly through the tattered sails; they flap ineffectively. Your boat has a leak, and you feel the weight of it taking on water. Your partner is trying to steer, but because you have no power, you find yourselves at the mercy of the currents as your boat drifts out of your control.

The power to sail with the wind is available to you, ready to be captured. The question of this chapter is this: What is the condition of your vessel and your sails? Are they whole, strong, shipshape? Are you and your partner ready to use your combined personal power? Are you both living in integrity? Or have you let your ship and sails become leaky, torn, and shredded by making ineffective agreements, not taking responsibility, not speaking the truth about how you feel or what you want, so that your energy just drains away? To really get moving in your relation-ship, you must eliminate your energy leaks and repair the rips of being out of integrity, while simultaneously letting your sails out to fully catch the wind, the full force of life energy that comes from being completely honest and transparent with your partner.

This examination of personal integrity is not about morality. It is not about hoping to be a "good person" or trying to "do the right thing." In fact, it is possible that your own personal compasses will steer you away from what you have believed to be the correct and appropriate way to live. Instead, these ideas are all about each of you coming into wholeness with yourselves so that you will have the power to sail in whatever direction you want to go.

As we move through the ways that people either maximize or diminish their own power, see if you can look at your own life with some level of detachment and a whole lot of compassion. These ideas are not meant to be one more way for you to judge and criticize yourself or your partner; they are simply invitations for you to mend the rips and seal the leaks of your life's energy. Together you and your partner can help each other harness the immensity of your full, co-creative power in building the life you really want.

The word "integrity" comes from the Latin "integer," meaning "whole," which you probably recognize from studying whole numbers back in grade school. Being in integrity is about living from one's wholeness, one's full self. Thoughts and feelings match words and deeds; the inner world of sensations and emotions is congruent with one's outer expression and behavior. Being out of integrity means that one's inner world and outer behavior are misaligned.

For example, let's say you bounced a check. To be in integrity, you would tell your partner while noticing your inner sensations: "My stomach feels clenched; I'm scared you won't trust me. I plan to call the bank in the morning and straighten this out." Then you would follow through until you had taken the actions that you said you had take. Being out of integrity? That could take lots of forms: not telling your partner; ignoring the problem as if it will go away; blaming your partner ("This never would have happened if you'd make more money!"); using drifts like drinking alcohol or being on the Internet to avoid talking about it; not tuning in to what you are really feeling but reacting with judgments instead ("I feel so stupid! I promise I'll never do this again!"). Notice how much simpler it is to be in integrity, though it can take courage to face what really is going on and to take the actions necessary to come back into wholeness.

Integrity lapses begin with our unwillingness to feel what we are really feeling. It is as if the wind is howling atop the deck and it feels too scary, too big, like it will toss us overboard and drown us, so we go below and hope it will all just blow over so we never have to face into it. Admitting our mistakes and dealing with the consequences; tuning in to the sensations of fluttering or clenching or tensing; having the nerve to say "No, I don't want to do that" when it would be so much easier to just go along ignoring the obvious—there are so many moments during a day when we can step into or out of integrity. Every time we choose wholeness with ourselves, however, it is like steering toward that powerful wind itself, maximizing its energy that will sweep us along to where we really want to go.

The moment of not facing our feelings head-on takes us right out of integrity. Without our attention, the energy of our unfelt feelings flows through our systems, creating havoc. Like water redirected from its natural course, this energy will seep out somewhere. As we found out in the last chapter, the energy of emotion must be expressed; its lack of direct expression means it is looking to be indirectly expressed. Along with creating unconscious behavior and body disease, one of humans' favorite ways to express this energy is by making up stories, either about others or about ourselves. The *unarguable* pure sensations and emotions become *arguable* projections. When we have distanced ourselves from our truth—that which we could swear to because we *know* what sensations we are having, what emotions they connect us with—the story takes on a life of its own. Often we use the story as an excuse not to take responsibility for what we are creating, seeing ourselves as simply along for the ride in the drama that is occurring all around us.

The crossroads moment of staying in or moving out of integrity, then, occurs as we decide whether or not to face the truth of our body sensations. This simple act has the potential of being diverted in so many ways, generally by what we're thinking or others are saying to us. Do any of these ideas sound familiar?

- I have no reason to be angry with them; they're doing the best they can.
- Nice people don't get mad.
- It wouldn't help if I said what I was feeling.
- I shouldn't feel scared; I'm supposed to be an adult!
- I can't feel sad; if I do, I'll never stop feeling that.
- If I feel too good, I'm just going to be disappointed.
- I can only feel sexual toward my partner.
- Good girls don't feel sexual or mad.
- Strong men don't feel scared or sad.
- If I feel my feelings, something terrible will happen: I might kill someone, have sex in the street, fall apart, go crazy, look weak, be vulnerable.

So the moment happens: the body sensations try to get our attention, and we decide to move away from them. That's when the unfelt emotion starts to make trouble. Diverted from our awareness, the emotional energy takes on a life of its own, leading to emotional withdrawal, projection, lies of omission, not following through with agreements, blame, and more. The farther we step away from the truth, the more we are out of integrity, and the more out of integrity we are, the more we distance ourselves, sometimes to the point that we lead separate, sometimes secret, lives.

> *Tom realized that he had a crush on his co-worker but knew his wife, Anne, would go through the roof if she knew about it. So he decided to keep it to himself, hoping it would pass. Then he found himself writing emails to his co-worker, thinking, "How could it hurt?" When he went on a business trip with the co-worker, he felt the thrill of the freedom of being out of Anne's reach, and let the relationship go a little further. . .*

> *Matt and David spent every other weekend with Matt's two teenaged kids from his former marriage. David dreaded this time and found himself counting the years until they'd be off to college. He complained about the kids, rolling his eyes when Matt would bring them up, but decided it would be too hurtful to say the whole truth: he'd been imagining how much easier it would be to have a partner who was unencumbered by such responsibilities.*

> *Patricia and Bonnie had a whirlwind and passionate beginning to their relationship. As time went on, though, they found themselves unable to contend with the variety of feelings (anger, sadness, fear) that emerged as the result of the intensity of their connection. After a while, these unfelt emotions created increasing distance between them, to the point that they found fewer and fewer ways to connect. They resigned themselves to giving up on their initial passion, believing that their choice was to live without it or find new partners.*

Withholding what is true creates the primary energetic clogs in intimacy, the cause behind the familiar lament, "I love my partner; I'm just not *in love* with him." Gay Hendricks[35] demonstrates this dynamic with this equation:

Anytime we withhold information from ourselves or from others,

Withhold ➤ Withdraw ➤ Project

we *must* withdraw; there is no choice. And once we have withdrawn, there is plenty of space from which to create stories, judgments, criticisms. The stories we tell ourselves over and over can really take hold, creating a framework for our dissatisfaction and negativity.

> *As Tom got further into the affair, his mind was filled with how Anne never did understand him and how his co-worker was much more of a natural fit.*

> *David, overhearing Matt's phone conversation with his daughter, thought, "These kids just take advantage of him; he's terrible at setting limits. I'm losing respect for him."*

> *Patricia had lunch with a friend; together, they commiserated about how passion inevitably dies out in a long-term relationship.*

When we withhold the truth from our intimate others, we will feel more and more distance from them. Within that distance is plenty of space to project, criticize, and judge, to come up with reasons to be unhappy—all because we didn't choose to speak our truth.

Plugging Power Leaks

Let's look at the main sources of power leaks and then examine how to plug them so that you can sail full-out. Get out your spyglass, climb up to the crow's nest, and take a sweeping look at your life. Take time to wonder what happens when you engage in these ways of being out of integrity, as you discover ways to move back in:

- Not telling the truth (including lies of omission)
- Blaming or not taking 100% responsibility

- Creating ineffective agreements
- Letting tasks or agreements remain incomplete
- Being out of alignment with your life

Each of the sections below explores what it means to be out of integrity and how you can come back into integrity—with yourself and with your partner.

Leak: Not Being Transparent
Plug: Impeccable Transparency

The opposite of not telling the whole truth is to be impeccably transparent. And what does that mean? We live in a culture that makes light of not telling the truth:

- A few white lies keep the romance alive.
- What he doesn't know won't hurt him.
- If I tell her, it will just hurt her feelings.
- It's better to tell them what they want to hear.

If you scrape away the guano, it's easy to see what is really going on: *If we tell the truth, we have to deal with the other person's reaction.* Keeping our feelings to ourselves can seem like an effective way to keep the peace—which can work, at least in the short term. If I don't say what is really going on for me, the other person will never have to know, so I won't have to face the reality of what my feelings are trying to tell me. However, the long-term effect of not speaking the truth is that emotions build up and become the bilge we described in Chapter 6. This withholding then results in withdrawing and projecting. When I withhold, I drive my energy down into my body (often creating physical symptoms) and use up lots of energy to keep myself from being aware of what I'm really creating. But at least my partner won't get upset!

Somehow that makes sense to us at the time.

The antidote to this lying pandemic—including the variety of forms it takes, such as concealing, telling partial truths, and creating lies of omission—is to simply speak what is true. It's pretty simple, isn't it? Yet people seem to get stuck on what it means to say the truth. So here's the bottom line, one that will sound familiar from Chapter 4: The truth is what is unarguable:

- Sensations: What's going on in your body
- Emotions: How you feel
- Inner knowing: What you want/don't want
- Noticing: Thoughts or images your mind is churning out

Remember how you can tell if you're saying something arguable: Someone is arguing with you. So you won't be saying things like this:

- You don't love me!
- You are so insensitive.
- I feel inadequate.
- I feel like you just don't care.

Notice that the first two are "you" statements: *You do this. You are that.* And notice that the last two start with "I feel" but don't conclude with a body sensation or an emotion. And the last one combines a misstated "I feel" with a blaming "you" statement. Blaming and making arguable statements lead to the defensive reactions we're trying not to activate by avoiding saying anything at all. Saying what is unarguable will allow you to connect with yourself and to extend a bridge of potential connection with your partner.

When you catch what is happening in that first moment your body is signaling you, it is very simple to speak what is true. Describing your body sensations, your emotions, and what you want (or don't want) creates a climate of impeccable transparency, where you're putting yourself right out there to be seen and known by your partner. Even if you have to backtrack through your stories and projections to the moment of withdrawal, back to finding the moment when you went out of integrity by not facing into what you were feeling—following this route will bring you back into instant connection with yourself and your partner. And you'll free up energy to get you and your intimacy moving again.

Because there is so much cultural pressure not to speak what is true, deciding to speak the truth begins with a commitment. You can make this commitment on your own, but speaking it directly to your partner will allow for a quantum leap in your communication together, as well as your potential for deep connection.

Exercise 1: Speaking the Truth

Make this commitment to your partner right now: *I commit to speaking the truth.*

Now go back to Shift Tool #3 in Chapter 4 and review what the unarguable truth sounds and looks like. It takes time to develop this skill, so give yourself plenty of practice as well as plenty of room to make mistakes.

* * *

Leak: Blaming
Plug: Step into Your Full Creativity

While not speaking the truth comes in first in creating huge energy leaks, blaming is a close second. There are different shades of blaming, from full-out blame, as in "You ruined my life!" to the more subtle forms of blame, as in "I'm not sure what's going on. Since I started seeing you, I just can't seem to get myself together." All blame is about looking outside of ourselves to explain why we're not getting what we want or why we're getting what we don't want.

Blaming is the energetic equivalent of sailing full-tilt and suddenly letting go of the sheet: the boat loses its source of power and completely stops. *You are the source of your own power.* When you place power outside of yourself in any way, that power is no longer available to you to move easily toward the life you want.

Do you remember the Drama Triangle from Chapter 3? The Bermuda Triangle of limbic reactivity, the sucking eddy into which many a relationship has been lost? The Drama Triangle thrives on blame. The Victim and the Hero blame the Villain:

Hero: "I can't believe how mean she is to you!"

Victim (sighing): "It's been that way for years."

The Villain blames the Victim: "What were you thinking?!" And the Victim blames himself or herself: "I know. I think there's really something wrong with me." Each position is out of calibration in terms of taking responsibility for creating the results of any situation:

- The Victim takes less than 100%: "I just don't know what happened."
- The Hero takes more than 100%: "No problem! I'll take care of it!"
- The Villain finds a way to do both simultaneously, using perceived slights to justify aggression: "I can't believe how you've betrayed me! Now I'm going after you for everything you're worth."

The adrenaline surges that accompany blaming give people a false sense of aliveness. In fact, for many people these surges are as good as it gets, especially when supplemented by caffeine, cocaine, or jumping out of planes. If life gets boring, creating a Drama Triangle pushes us into overdrive once again.

The antidote to blaming is—you guessed it!—taking 100% responsibility. Always. No matter what. Sure, it looks like your partner's fault for not depositing your check or your co-worker's fault for failing to complete the project, or the government's for making you pay taxes. Take a moment to think of your own examples of whom or what you might want to blame for what is not working in your life. What do you notice is happening in your body? Maybe there's that first little bit of self-righteous surge, but then what? Can you feel your energy starting to sag? Here is what taking 100% responsibility sounds like:

- "I wonder how I didn't clearly communicate about getting that money into our account."
- "I see how I never followed up with you to see the status of that project."
- "I'm choosing to live in this country, and as a citizen, paying taxes is one of my ways of supporting it."

Each time you choose to shift out of blame and into responsibility, you tap into an endless energy source. In fact, making the move to view oneself as the source, not the victim, of one's life circumstances really is the channel out of Reactive Brain (Below the Line) and into Creative Brain (Above the Line) asking the fundamental question "How am *I* creating this?" opens a whole new world of exploring what is going on beneath your own surface.

Staying committed to claiming yourself as the source of whatever happens in your life can be particularly challenging when you cannot see any apparent connection between what you want to create and the results you are getting. The idea of being "at the effect of" life or others can feel so seductive. However, these are the times that it can be even more freeing and empowering to steer into the channel of Willingness and cross into the world Above the Line. When you look to yourself as the source—when you take 100% responsibility—you free up tremendous, previously untapped, creative energy with which to see the situation more expansively and dream up new solutions. In short, taking 100% responsibility means claiming 100% of your own power.

Exercise 2: *Shifting into 100% Responsibility*

Do you remember the Wondering Shift Tool from Chapter 4, where you made a vibrating "hmmm" sound to create a sense of openness to what you don't already know? Use that tool here when you are trying out these questions.

1. Choose an issue that you feel stuck about, one where you could make a clear case for being the victim. It might be a struggle you're having with your partner or a sense that you're not where you want to be in your life.
2. Now answer these questions, listing as many answers as you can:
    - How am *I* creating this?
    - How am *I* keeping this going?
    - What am *I* getting out of things being this way?[36]
3. Notice that these powerful, compelling, even provocative questions require you to go down deep for answers.

This approach of stepping into your own creativity is about looking at what you are doing, which can be a lot harder than seeing what everybody else is doing. Keep trying; answering these questions will instantly give you back your power and get you moving again.

* * *

Leak: Making Agreements That Don't Work
Plug: Make Powerful Agreements

Now aim your spyglass at another area of your life, again with lots of spaciousness and breath and compassion: the area of agreements. Broken agreements tear the sails of your partnership, leaking energy with each, "Oh, I forgot" or "You said you'd remind me" or "I'll try harder next time." Our ability to make powerful agreements and keep them is key to building trust.

Stepping into making great agreements will test your mettle about speaking the truth; we often seem to prefer placating someone—"OK, sure, I'll go see your family"—to stepping into the fire of speaking what we really want—"I don't want to go."

Making an effective agreement means that you and your partner:

- Agree to what you each will do.
- Feel good about what you've agreed to.
- Follow through easily on the agreement.

The ability to make effective agreements is key to feeling powerful together. Developing this ability means you don't have to use up your energy worrying about or tracking whether your partner (or you) are doing what you said you would do. And working together to come up with how you can both get what you really want supports the vision of you both being fully expressed in your relationship.

In Chapter 5 we considered how each person can get what she or he wants, which is really the prerequisite for making powerful agreements. Let's go over this skill again, this time in the context of agreements. Making agreements is the perfect place for falling into the old habit of blame. It is likely that you are in one of two camps:

- You're the person who keeps agreements but is frustrated with others' inability to follow through.

- You're the person other folks complain about: "Why is he always late?!" or "When is she going to pay back the money she borrowed?!"

It doesn't matter who has the moral high ground on this issue. No matter whether you keep agreements that others break or you are notoriously bad at following through—even if you manage not to get caught—the end result is the same: you are creating an energy leak by making ineffective agreements. If you are in the first camp, you have to monitor others to make sure they follow through, manipulating and controlling them to do what they said they would. If you are in the second camp, you have to watch your back, avoiding phone calls, not opening mail, trying not to think about what you said you'd do. And then, of course, for each there's the moment of having to confront the issue, when you can either self-righteously attack the other for breaking the agreement or you sheepishly withstand someone else's reprimand.

Here's a concept that will free you from fighting about agreements: Taking 100% responsibility means *both* people are responsible for a broken agreement. Making an agreement is a team sport: when an agreement is broken, the team loses; when an agreement works for everyone, the team wins.

The ground rules for making effective agreements[37] are so simple you might not even see them as "rules":

- Make only those agreements you want to make (guided
- by your Internal Compass).
- Don't make agreements you don't want to make (using your Internal Compass without fail).
- Renegotiate the agreements you want to change or agreements you no longer want to have.[38]

Vagueness or fuzziness about an issue is a signal that an agreement needs to be made; resentment will tell you when you probably should have made an agreement a while ago.

Stepping into the New Paradigm

Are you ready to take another step toward filling your sails and sealing your leaks? Then welcome to the world of creating powerful agreements. We practiced this before, but let's reiterate: A powerful agreement is one in which everybody gets everything they want.

Notice what happens with this kind of agreement. First and foremost, the agreement is easy to keep. No policing is required; neither person will rebel with passive-aggressive behavior. When you get what you want from an agreement, you feel energized and motivated to follow through. You're not compromising, giving up half of what you want and expecting the other person to give up half of what he or she wants so that you each end up half-heartedly making yourselves follow through with something neither of you really wants. You don't have to keep score, trying to keep everything even and fair: who is giving up what and when; who is getting what she or he wants. Instead, the agreement is a co-creation, a moment of two or more people going beyond what they have known before, creating a new world together.

Remember, to make such powerful agreements, you need two of your tools: your Relationship Map (to help you stay Above the Line) and your Internal Compass (to steer toward what you really want).

First look at the Relationship Map and notice how two people interact according to whether they are Above the Line or Below the Line. Two Reactive Brains will naturally see the other as a competitor in a world where there isn't enough to go around. One will try to dominate the other, who might initially be willing to submit ("agree") but who is eventually likely to sabotage the agreement through resistance ("Oh, I forgot!") that then requires the first person to nag. This is the perfect storm within which to cultivate power struggles, where one person can take on the parental qualities of the Hero ("I know; let's have a budget!")

or the Villain ("I can't believe you bounced a check AGAIN!"), while the other digs deeper into the childish hold of the Victim ("I don't know how that happened. I'll try harder next time! Really I will!").

As you check your Internal Compass, notice that in the world of Reactive Brain, what you each want gets cast aside in the push to keep what you have and to make sure you don't get what you don't want. The characteristic quality of contraction turns agreements into an issue of not losing rather than agreements in which each feels like a winner.

Two Creative Brains, on the other hand, have the opportunity to use their relationship as a glorious playground of wonder. Freed from the contraction of being competitors for scarce resources and the tension of who is dominant and who is submissive, each person opens up access to interesting, previously unconsidered possibilities that can be tossed back and forth until a new possibility excites both people. Each person can bring out his or her Internal Compass and follow it as a guide toward solutions that come closer and closer to the true north of expressing essence. Agreements, then, carry excitement that goes far beyond how to manage money or when to have dinner. They become an expression of each person's uniqueness.

Exercise Bonus: Everybody Gets What They Want

Now that you understand more about the importance of making great agreements, go back and try out Exercise 2 in Chapter 5 again.

Exercise 3: Agreements Inventory

Take a few minutes to consider where you stand with agreements in your life. Are you willing to be even more powerful by sealing your leaks and filling your sails? Then make some lists:

- What agreements do you need to make?

- Wonder about any area in which you feel vague, fuzzy, or resentful with the people in your life.
- What agreements did you make that you didn't want to make?
- Check into anything you've been avoiding doing or following through with.
- Finish the steps needed to complete outstanding agreements—and take them!

From the lists you just made, create an action plan for all of the agreements you will make, clearly terminate, or renegotiate.

* * *

Leak: Incompletion
Plug: Create Completion

From up there in that lofty vantage point of the crow's nest, take a breath and wonder where in your life you have created incompletion—those dangling annoyances that you would rather avoid than deal with. Do you have outstanding bills? Credit cards that you can barely pay the minimum balance on? Are there people you have avoided because there are truths you have not wanted to speak? Actions you said you would take but never did? And how about the past: Have you fully expressed anything you have kept bottled up in you from something that happened in your past (which could be thirty years ago or this morning)?

Typically, incompletion shows up where energy flow is an issue. Here are a few examples:

- Money

    This could be money we owe or money others owe us; actions we avoid taking to create more security in our lives, like having the right insurance or creating wills or other estate completions; being fully aware of how money is flowing in or out; being in alignment with our true calling.

- Relationships

    What has not yet been spoken that is creating an energetic disconnection in your relationships? What emotions have you avoided feeling that are keeping you disconnected from those you used to feel intimate with?

- Physical World

    What actions do you need to take in the material world around you, like your car, your home, or your body? Clearing away physical clutter, repairing what is broken, and streamlining processes are all effective ways to increase the flow of energy around and through you.

- Creativity

    Whether or not you consider yourself a creative person, you create something every time you make a choice. Giving yourself the time to complete creative projects will open up the flow for more creativity. And notice how you might use your incomplete to-do list to never let yourself try out new ways to be creative.

- Expression

    Words we haven't spoken, experiences from the past that we've never let ourselves fully know about, and emotions we haven't fully processed can all create energetic blocks in our bodies and in our lives.

Incompletion occurs for some of the same reasons we accumulate emotional bilge: we would rather do anything than face the discomfort of what we experience when we think about the area that needs attention. Pulling out our favorite drifts (those things we do instead of feeling what we're feeling) can provide so much relief—even if it is just momentary—that we often choose to watch TV instead of creating a financial plan, or have a drink instead of calling a family member to speak the truth to, or do a little more "retail therapy" rather than face issues from the past. We become so concerned with trying to stay afloat that we don't notice the water filling our hulls or how our sails aren't really pulling us forward anymore.

Creating completion wherever we find incompletion removes these blocks, clears away the reasons for withdrawing (and the associated energy leaks), and allows us to get moving again.

Exercise 4: Incompletion Inventory

Consider each area in your life and list the completions you need to make and the date by which you are willing to take action. You can do this exercise in a table located in Appendix A, or you can download a copy from the Duffle Bag at www.JuliaColwell.com.

These are the main areas of incompletion to consider:

- Money—What you owe or others owe you; actions you avoid taking to create more security in your life; being fully aware of how money is flowing in or out; being in alignment with one's true calling.
- Relationships—What needs to be spoken, to whom; emotions you are having that you haven't yet faced.
- Physical World—Car, home, body, physical clutter.
- Creativity—Creative projects, letting yourself be creative.
- Expression—Words you haven't spoken, experiences from the past to be faced, emotions you haven't processed.

* * *

Leak: Being Out of Alignment in Your Life
Plug: Live Your True Life

Well, Sailor, you're probably about ready to climb down the rigging. Even swabbing the deck might look pretty good by now. But wait! There's one last area to scan for yourself, one more place from which to gauge your level of integrity. This one really requires a bird's-eye view of your whole life. It comes up from that question in Chapter 5: *Are you willing to live the life you really want?* Because notice this: The degree to which you are off course from this question, how far away your current life is from the one you really want to live, is the amount of energy you are leaking every day. It isn't possible to be whole and live a life that doesn't match who you are.

Your willingness to even ask this question promotes you to captain of your ship. Say you have a "good job" that pays the bills but you feel exhausted and drained by this job: Are you willing to consider that your heart's desire might be to write or to work with your hands in the dirt? To change the course of your life can be frightening and difficult to consider, especially if you are blown far off course. However, as you make choices that bring your life closer and closer to expressing your essential self, you will find yourself coming into alignment with your own power, and you will be better able to access the winds blowing around you, multiplying your experiences of living in ease and flow. Rather than attempt to sail across your own inner currents, you will find the wind at your back, blowing into your whole, unfurled sails.

Relationship, of course, makes this more challenging. Creating lives where both people are in full alignment with their own essence while staying on the same ship means broadening your abilities to live together from Creative Brain while steering toward the same vision. Ultimately, there is nothing more invigorating than sailing along, knowing that the course is true and the sails are full, with each person feeling seen, heard, and completely expressed.

Try out that vision: Imagine being in a relationship in which there is little or no energy leakage. Each person can speak and feel what is true at any given moment, skillfully surfing the waves of emotion and clearing out bilge. Both of you step into taking 100% responsibility for any result, so together you surmount difficulties and celebrate successes. You make powerful, inspired, co-creative agreements, which means you each are getting everything you really want, and the blend of your essential selves is apparent in your agreements. You both quickly take care of any incompletion so that neither of you spends energy policing the other. And your relationship itself is the vehicle that carries both of you toward the fulfillment and expression of your highest selves.

Are you interested in sailing toward that brave new world?

Exercise 5: Creating the Life You Really Want to Live

For this exercise, do not give in to your problem-solving brain's desire to figure out *how* you could do this or to come up with a solution of any kind. In your mind, create the vision and allow yourself to simply be in the wonder of how such a life might come about. Got paper and something to write with? Go!

- Imagine your perfect day. Starting with the specifics of waking up (when would that be?), how would you spend your day? What would you choose to do? Who would you be spending your time with? Map out what this would look like with as much detail as you can imagine.
- Now try out this commitment again:

    I commit to living the life I *really want*.

If you do this exercise with your partner, share what you each came up with and decide if you would like to create the kind of relation-*ship* big enough to carry you both to the lives you really want.

Points to Steer By

- To really get moving in your relationship, you must eliminate your energy leaks and repair the rips of being out of integrity while simultaneously letting your sails out to fully catch the wind, the full force of life energy that comes from being completely honest and transparent with your partner.
- Being in integrity is about living from one's wholeness, one's full self.
- Integrity lapses begin with our unwillingness to feel what we are really feeling. The crossroads moment of staying in or moving out of integrity occurs as we decide whether or not to face into the truth of our body sensations.
- Withholding what is true creates the primary energetic clogs in intimacy.
- The main reason we withhold the truth is this: If we tell the truth, we have to deal with the other person's reaction.
- 100% Responsibility = 100% Power.
- The ability to make effective agreements is key to feeling powerful together; an effective agreement is one in which everybody gets everything they want.
- Taking 100% responsibility means both people are responsible for a broken agreement.
- The characteristic quality of contraction turns agreements into an issue of not losing rather than agreements in which each feels like a winner.
- How far away your current life is from the one you really want to live, plus the other ways you are out of integrity, is the amount of energy you are leaking every day.

- It isn't possible to be whole and live a life that doesn't match who you are.

II

Navigating the Open Sea

> *"Wouldst thou," so the helmsman answered, / "Learn the secrets of the sea? / Only those who brave its dangers / Comprehend its mystery!*
>
> ~ HENRY WADSWORTH LONGFELLOW

Aye, Matey! It's time to pack up your duffle bag and ready yourself for the challenges of the open sea of relation-ship. Have you got your tools?

- Inner Map
- Pressure Gauge
- Relationship Map
- Shift Tools
- Internal Compass
- Bilge Pump
- Leak Plugger Kit

They will all help you, whether you hit a storm, run aground, have to steer through the rocks, get becalmed, come upon sea monsters—or you just want to sail full-out. You can't learn until you're there, so let's go!

See Appendix A for a quick reference to the tools.

8

Running Aground — Moving Again

Sail forth—steer for the deep waters only,
Reckless, O soul, exploring, I with thee, and thou with me,
For we are bound where mariner has not yet dared to go,
And we will risk the ship, ourselves and all.
                                        ~ Walt Whitman
No matter what, something will always happen. Always.
                                ~ Kathlyn Hendricks, Ph.D.

You have made it this far through *The Relationship Ride*; clearly you have the mettle for a life of adventure. You could have chosen to keep your relationships ordinary and dim your aliveness by playing out your old unconscious patterns. Instead, you are stepping into the excitement of being fully present in this very moment. Your willingness to be authentic and live in integrity opens you to full participation with whatever life has to offer. As you sail along, you will find that you continually discover new treasures and rewards.

Sailing out of the safe harbor of the familiar means you are choosing a life of unpredictability and challenge. As you read in earlier chapters, in life and relationship something always happens. You start moving, maybe find your rhythm, feel the glide of being in ease and flow—and something comes along to disrupt that. Of course, this makes the ride much more interesting, though people seem to view this as a failure, having some idea that if we and our relationships were "functional" (instead of the dreaded "dysfunctional"), we would keep moving smoothly, no matter what came along.

The question, then, isn't how to keep life from happening; the question is what you will do when "something" happens. When there are two or more people involved in a challenging circumstance, there are exponentially more opportunities to learn how to effectively respond. If each person understands that relationship offers endless chances for old patterns to emerge and be shifted, as well as opportunities for responding completely differently, the voyage of connection can take on a tone of an ongoing adventure.

As we discovered earlier, the main danger for couples is that they will run aground and sink the relationship through power struggle. Many problems in relationships, including affairs, addictions, numbing out, and distancing result from trying to resurrect good feelings from the frustration of power struggles. This pattern—getting stuck, finding no satisfying way through, and turning to other outlets to feel better—often leads people to end relationships. Understanding how this pattern works is key to knowing how to change it. This chapter gives you practice in running aground in struggle and then getting yourselves moving again.

Running Aground

Take a look at the Relationship Map again (if you'd like, you can download it from the Duffle Bag at www.JuliaColwell.com). Notice the Drama Triangle Below the Line at the Bermuda Triangle of relationships. This Drama Triangle is the blueprint for power struggles. As you orient yourself to the three routes into the triangle—Victim, Hero, and Villain—notice that once you enter this zone, steering your way out again can be tricky. A Reactive Brain creates something like an energy vortex that pulls all nearby beings in with it, even if it means the doom of all.

So here is how power struggles typically get going, when couples run aground or maybe even hit the rocks: The unpredictability of the "some-things" that happen triggers our fear of being out of control. The Reactive Brain lurches toward the illusion that control can be re-established, which usually means either assuming the dominant role of controller or submitting to someone else stepping in to take control. The chaotic moments that can occur between something happening and two (or more) Reactive Brains vying for control are when power struggles are most likely to occur. These struggles can take on a life of their own as the tug-of-war for control stimulates our threatened animal selves, who are likely to snarl, go for the jugular, roll over, or be equally animal-like.

The challenge during these unstable moments is to switch out of the basic instinct to hang on to control and then to shift into the arena of Creative Brain. Here, instead of internally grasping onto a controlled reality (also known as "being right,") it is possible to step into and co-create a much bigger field of potential.

Keep in mind that our Reactive Brains—which focus on ensuring our survival no matter what the cost—have been successful. Otherwise, you wouldn't be sitting here reading this book. Having a system of rapidly responding to threat has meant that humans could ward off danger and continue to generate and evolve our species; that remains true, though mostly our Reactive Brains are sounding the alarm for a ferocious tiger that doesn't exist. However, the very response that helps us to deal with short-term threat is also the response that creates power struggles.

Our reactivity—which leads us to immediately contract into the instinctive safety of a dominance/submission hierarchy—creates the perfect storm of conditions for frustration and stuckness in trying to resolve issues. To take the next step in our evolution, we must forge co-creative partnerships between equals.

Ironically, Western culture is imbued with the "romance of rescuing,"[39] a main path into power struggle. Being steeped in endless stories of the brave hero who rescues the poor, victimized damsel in distress from the evil villain can lure unsuspecting couples into using the Drama Triangle as the basis for their relationships. Not knowing this, many people aspire to become better heroes, believing it to be a morally advanced way to live and the prototype for what a good partner should look like.

> *Joan met Frank in college. She was from a family that was financially well-off, even after her parents divorced; his family was violent and often precipitously close to bankruptcy. Joan was really attracted to Frank's "bad boy" image and the depth she sensed that lay beneath his toughness. She vowed to love him more than he'd been loved before.*

> *Matt met David soon after David came out of rehab for alcoholism. Even though David knew his program recommended he stay out of relationship for at least a year, Matt reassured David that he could be patient and supportive through David's recovery.*

> *Patricia was Bonnie's boss when they fell in love. Bonnie felt secure and safe around Patricia, who was fifteen years older and dazzled to discover a partner so young and vibrant. Since Patricia made quite a bit more money than Bonnie, she had no problem paying Bonnie's way for dinner out and fabulous vacations. Bonnie moved into Patricia's beautiful home.*

Few people can maintain the Hero stance over time.

Consider the iconic saying "He ain't heavy, he's my brother." Though this might be true at first, after awhile he's going to get heavy. And whoever is carrying him might start to wonder why the heck he can't just walk on his own two feet. Thus, what begins in an impulse of romanticized love ("I'll be there for you forever! You can always count on me!!" declares the Hero, to the adoring "Oh, my hero!" from the Victim) simply cannot last. The Hero, by definition, takes on a parental role, first as the nurturing parent trying to hold onto being "nice," inevitably becoming the critical parent as the Victim becomes more and more child-like.

Finally, inevitably, the Hero becomes a Villain. While these roles might feel familiar (especially since they are the templates of relationship for every one of us), over time adults get tired of either having to be the parent of a grown adult or being a grown adult in the child position. What started out feeling romantic now feels like an albatross.

> *Joan viewed Frank as a "work-in-progress." Because of his background of poverty, she saw it as her responsibility to help him learn good money management.*

> *She monitored his spending and made sure he followed the budget she set up. Frank went along with Joan, believing that she understood money better. He did have occasional lapses—a few bounced checks, running out of money before payday—but each time Joan pointed out these broken agreements, he vowed to Joan that he'd do better. He also started using his own credit card, the one with the statement that got sent to his work.*

> *Matt watched over David, making sure he made it to AA meetings. To be supportive, Matt didn't drink for a while. Then he realized he missed it, and started ordering alcohol when they went out with friends. David would just have to deal with it. David wondered why he was feeling increasingly tense. He began to miss meetings. His work schedule was tight, and he had to have some fun sometime, right?*

> *Bonnie was grateful for Patricia's financial support. She could finally leave that old job and go back to school! Patricia, wanting to use her money wisely, counseled Bonnie about what school she thought she should attend and which profession she would do best at. Bonnie accepted the wisdom of Patricia's experience. She wondered why she didn't unpack her own things,*

though. Then there was the day she left the stove on—but there was only smoke damage, thank God.

By the way, these roles aren't gender-connected; any one of us can feel compelled to be a Hero to anyone else, as well as to want to be rescued. And they can happen concurrently in the same relationship, where one person is a Hero and the other a Victim in specific situations. This drift into creating rigid roles of parent and child leads to many difficulties in relationships. In fact, what might seem to be just "who people are" can actually be a byproduct of making these roles rigid.

In the sections below, see if you recognize yourself in any of these Drama Triangle roles:

- Parent role—which can be divided into the Nurturing Parent (Hero) and the Critical Parent (Villain)
- Child role, also known as the Victim[40]

Long-Term Characteristics of the Parent (Hero/Villain) Role

While the impulse to take care of, support, and nurture others is one of the more exemplary aspects of being human, these are all qualities of parenting. Parenting qualities are essential for raising children; however, they don't cultivate fertile ground for co-creative relationships. Parents, by definition, control.

Eventually, those who are being controlled—whether it is a growing child or a partner—resist. This resistance keeps the controller from getting what she or he wants. And not getting what we want is the definition of frustration.

The experience of frustration is what turns the Hero (Nurturing Parent) into the Villain (Critical Parent). The controller's directives might start with a sweet tone, but if the controller is thwarted—when things don't go the way the controller wants—these directions take on increasing amounts of anger as the controller tries to push through the obstacle. "Honey, would you mind not being late?" becomes "I thought you said you wouldn't be late," which turns into "I can't believe you were late again!" to "I am SICK of you being late" and the ultimate "You are an irresponsible JERK!" When we try to control someone else, we start on the "nice" side but eventually flip over to "mean." And this human tendency to shift from being nice to being mean is not very different from the alpha dog who keeps order in the pack by first nudging the subordinate, then baring his teeth, then growling, and finally biting and going for the throat. Bosses, military officers, and parents all know how to keep order in the ranks by increasing their aggression towards subordinates who don't obey. When lives and fortunes are at stake, humans are typically ready to make the trade-off of potentially angering the subordinate to maintain control.

Staying in this controlling position, however, comes at a price. Because other beings have a natural inclination to want to control their own destinies, the controller who wants to maintain this position when encountering the ongoing frustration of resistance will take on certain characteristics. To stay in this Power-Over[41] position, the controller must be tough and not display softness. Thus, these people might appear to have particular characteristics. They can seem:

- Directive
- Right
- Angry (not scared, sad, or appearing in any way to be "vulnerable")
- Irritable (because they dare not access any of their other feelings)
- Burdened
- Over-responsible
- Overactive
- Clear about what they want
- Aggressive
- Demanding about getting their needs met (including the need for sexual expression)

- Critical
- Anxious (in an agitated way)
- Resentful
- Exhausted (from taking on too much)
- Domineering
- Prone to addictions (to keep up their tough veneer)
- Contemptuous

A fascinating aspect of the Power-Over position is that it explains many of the qualities we have ascribed to gender. We tend to think of the following as male attributes: having a sense of personal entitlement; taking up verbal space; interrupting; being directive, ambitious, and aggressive; tending toward non-monogamy. However, these are all traits that arise out of being Power Over, and they dissolve once the power difference shifts or disappears.[42]

Long-Term Characteristics of the Child (Victim) Role

Now let's shift focus to the person who allows himself or herself to be controlled, the one who is in the Power-Under position. Taking on the subordinate position might come from a conscious expectation—for example, from the belief that it is religiously correct to obey one's husband. More often taking on this position is simply an unconscious slide into a role that feels safe and comfortable. Choosing to give up one's self for financial, social, and emotional security and the safety of connection is so ingrained that anyone who has uttered the phrase "I don't care; whatever you want" will recognize this choice. Giving up control can feel like a relief, that sense of "let someone else be responsible for a while." And that yearning to be taken care of still exists in all of us, no matter how old we are. Darkness, illness, even being cold stimulates an instinctual need to reach out for nurturance.[43]

The initial compromise of trading self for security can start a trajectory toward long-term problems. Adults must have a self. Even if we choose to try to make our self diminish, it will inevitably push back for expression. Like a balloon that is being shoved under water, self wants to pop back to the surface. It takes a lot of energy to counteract this drive for identity. The incremental steps toward diminishing ourselves to keep the peace simply cannot continue without leading to a variety of issues. Low energy, poor self esteem, low libido, inability to make choices and decisions, exhaustion, and depression can be the result of trying to keep self at bay.

Just as the alpha dog knows how to nudge, bark, and bite to stay dominant, submissive pack animals know how to behave. Rolling over, showing one's soft parts, drooping, and collapsing are all familiar behaviors for humans and other animals who want to placate the dominant one. Put these together and you get characteristics of Power Under that are easy to spot. People who are in the Power-Under position can seem to be:

- Compliant ("Yes, Dear.")
- Wrong
- Placating ("Whatever you want.")
- Giving up of self ("I don't know what I want.")
- Under-responsible
- Unreliable about agreements
- Helpless
- Childlike—as if they refuse to grow up
- Accepting of not being respected
- Collapsed
- Apologetic
- Passive-aggressive
- Depressed
- Having a low sex drive
- Anxious (in an amorphous, vague way)
- Sullen
- Withdrawn

- Stonewalling
- Prone to addictions (to feel better)
- Accepting of contempt or contemptuous towards self

As with Power-Over, Power-Under characteristics have been masked as gender differences. Women's tendency to ask questions, qualify their statements, use "uptalk" (the lilting questioning at the end of a statement), not use declarative statements, view taking care of their own needs as "selfish," and diminish their accomplishments can all be explained simply as ways people behave when they sense themselves to be Power Under.[44]

Small differences in power at the start of a relationship can lead to increasingly polarized roles over time. In the throes of the romance of the rescue, a relationship can start with the powerful Hero saving the helpless Victim. Eventually, however, the Victim's self will have to re-emerge, which looks like the Victim beginning to resist. Frustrated by this new resistance, the Hero starts sounding more and more like a Villain, pushing for further collapse by the Victim. Then the backlash begins. As the Victim's self leaks out through more resistance and passive aggressive—and ultimately aggressive—behavior, the Hero-Villain might finally give up into collapse, flipping the whole dynamic. (This is also known as "fighting for the Victim position."[45]) As the struggle for dominance continues, positions tend to become even more polarized and rigidified into the Hero, Victim, and Villain roles and associated qualities. This rigidifying gets really confusing as each person starts to believe that he or she really is defined by all of those aspects instead of realizing that roles have taken over.

> *Joan and Frank started fighting about money. She was angry because he kept breaking his agreements about not bouncing checks and spending frivolously. He was tired of having her look over his shoulder all the time. Wasn't he an adult? With his own job?? Frank began staying out later with his old friends, occasionally buying a round for the house. His credit card balance*

was creeping up, but it didn't matter. Joan would never find out. Joan started to feel increasingly unhappy with Frank's behavior and began complaining to friends about how men just never grow up. They gave up talking about money, since the conversations went nowhere.

Because Matt and David loved to have dinner parties and go out with friends, they agreed that it wouldn't be a problem for David to drink socially. They knew he could control it. One day David drove home drunk and they got into a big fight. Matt told David he'd better get his drinking under control or else, that he wasn't going to be with a drunk like his father. They scuffled as David tried to stomp away and Matt tried to stop him, pushing each other and landing a few punches. David broke away and went back to the bar, where he felt free.

Bonnie excelled as a student. When she got home, though, she and Patricia seemed to be fighting more. The fights became predictable, usually focused on how Bonnie wasn't home enough and Patricia's resentment about doing more than her share of the housework.

They both were tired a lot, kind of numbed out, but each figured that was just how life goes. Patricia wished they'd have sex more often, but Bonnie just wasn't interested. They tried to talk about it but got nowhere. Patricia began to worry about being too old for Bonnie. Meanwhile, Bonnie wondered if she had a problem with low sexual desire. Then one day at school, she met Danny and felt those old feelings rushing back in. She knew not to mention Danny to Patricia, especially as the crush intensified. She asked Danny to go out with her for coffee. Patricia could feel Bonnie getting more distant; she comforted herself with TV dramas and chocolate chip cookies.

The irony of power struggles is that neither person feels powerful. The one in the Power-Over position feels frustrated and thwarted by Power Under's resistance. Power Under has lost his sense of self and, over time, his ability to identify what he wants. While there might seem to be a winner, in fact, everyone loses in power struggles.

Two (or more) Reactive Brains ignite struggles that can escalate through domination moves and countermoves: going for the throat through contempt and criticism, defensively striking out, using shaming and humiliation ("low blows"), and entering a reality where the conflict appears to be a fight for survival. This resonance chamber of reactivity can lead to continued escalation (which is generally how domestic violence occurs). Alternatively, one or the other person might give up power by collapsing, withdrawing, or stonewalling. Either way, the issue remains unresolved. Ultimately it can seem like the only way to get moving again is to get away from the other person. Such distancing is reinforcing when each person feels much better when alone or around people other than the partner; then it is quite logical that the partner is the problem. Affairs, secrets, drifting, and addictions are often desperate attempts to resurrect a positive sense of self.

Getting Moving Again

Now that you have studied the Bermuda Triangle of relationships very carefully, you know your way around the vortex that has the potential to pull you down and under, get you really stuck. It is time to practice what it is like to have real power. You have got all you need to steer through the difficult waters of potential power struggle: your maps, Pressure Gauge, Shift Tools, Internal Compass, Bilge Pump, and Leak Plugger Kit. Let's get going to move out of the trance of hierarchy and Power Over/Power Under and into the co-creative sphere of Power With. Here you can experience not only the endless energy of your own ability to create the life you want but also the rich potential of combining your power with that of your partner, allowing the two of you not just to sail but to soar into the vastness of possibility.

The territory of Power With is the next stage of human evolution. Here we all get to be as big as possible, living our true gifts without threatening anyone else. There is no need for some to dominate and others to submit; we each can express our true, essential nature and be heard, known, and valued. No one controls anyone else; instead, we all get to tune in to and express our deepest inner truths. Everyone can speak clearly about what she or he wants, and there is plenty of creative space to come up with solutions that include all of these wants. Competition transforms to teamwork as it becomes clear that what benefits one, benefits all. The truth is a tool for ongoing intimate emotional connection. Energy flies freely.

Communication in Power With is easy and flowing. Our ideas build off of each other, allowing us access to and discovery of previously unknown possibilities. We each state clearly what we want while listening deeply to the other's desires. We have mutual respect for each other while we mutually take responsibility. We make impeccable agreements that are easy to keep because they reflect our true desires. Overall, there is a sense of play, possibility, curiosity, creativity, and abundance in how we interact with each other.

How does that sound to you? Are you ready to experience this new world of possibility? As with any seaworthy vessel, there are many tools and instruments to master that will allow you to steer through storms, catch the best wind, and respond no matter what the weather. With such a long list as this, you can focus on one or another at different times on your way to becoming the master of your life. Take a moment to examine the collection of instruments and tools that you have been assembling (see Appendix A for a quick reference to the tools):

- Inner Map

   Locates you according to how contracted or expanded your current state is. Where are you currently on your Inner Map?

- Pressure Gauge

   Measures how immobilized/mobilized or calm you are, so that

you can locate yourself more accurately on the Inner Map. What are your readings?

- Relationship Map

    Locates your current state and your partner's, including whether you are in the Drama Triangle. Where are the two of you currently on the Relationship Map?

- Shift Tools

    To help you get moving across the channel from Below the Line to Above the Line. Includes Noticing, Being Present, Speaking the Unarguable Truth, Wondering, Breathing, Moving, Playing, Making It Bigger, Creatively Expressing, Appreciating, Loving What Is.

- Internal Compass

    Locates what you want and what you don't want. What do you really want?

- Bilge Pump

    Process for pumping out your old, contracted emotional energy. What emotions do you need to feel so that they can dissipate?

- Leak Plugger Kit

    Checks where you have integrity leaks. Where are you out of integrity?

First let's practice with the people we have been getting to know from the examples. Let's use what you have learned to help them steer away from the rocks, help them get moving again. To begin, let's take some readings with Joan and Frank to see how they are doing with their tools. Notice that these readings are about their most difficult interactions; it is unlikely that they are always in these states.

- Pressure Gauge

  Joan is mobilized; Frank is immobilized. Both are Below the Line, in contraction. Their thoughts about the other are negative overall, and they each keep generating contracted responses from the other.

- Inner Map

  Joan is in Anger; Frank feels Fear and Shame.

- Relationship Map

  Joan is stuck at Hero-Villain; Frank is stuck at Victim. These roles flip when Joan complains about Frank and Frank has critical thoughts about Joan.

- Bilge Pump

  Both are pretty backed up!

- Leak Plugger Kit

  Both Joan and Frank are out of integrity in a variety of ways. They aren't making effective agreements; they aren't speaking the real truth, the unarguable truth; they are stuck in blame and not taking responsibility for how they are creating the issues.

- Shift Tools

    Neither is using any Shift Tools; both are drifting.

- Internal Compass

    Both have lost sight of what they really want, focusing instead on moment-to-moment cravings.

So, what shall we have them do? How about using some Shift Tools? Let's lay them out so you can see them all:

- Noticing
- Being Present
- Speaking the Unarguable Truth
- Wondering
- Breathing
- Moving
- Playing
- Making It Bigger
- Expressing Creatively
- Appreciating
- Loving What Is

Let's also have the Bilge Pump, Leak Plugger Kit, and Internal Compass ready to help them move out old emotional energy and make better agreements. Each will choose moves to shift her or his individual emotional energy before working together to shift the emotional energy in their relationship. Notice that the examples below make it sound like these shifts happen fast; in fact, there is no hurry. Each person has her or his own speed moving from Reactive to Creative Brain.

(When you apply these tools to yourself and your relationship, give yourself the gift of following your own internal rhythm.)

Let's ask Joan if she's willing. Until she decides she's willing to cross the channel, nothing else will happen. Assuming that she would love to shift, that she's really tired of being stuck, we'll now guide her to tune in to her inner world. Joan *notices* a tightness in her gut and her jaw. We ask her to *be present* with that tightness, to really experience it. Then we ask her to *say something unarguable*; she says, "I notice tightness in my gut and my jaw; I feel scared and angry." We ask her to get out her Bilge Pump and ride the waves of her emotional energy, letting herself feel as afraid and angry as she feels until these emotions have passed through her completely.

Now we direct her to *wonder* about this issue; she says, "I wonder why I can only see what is negative in Frank. I wonder how I could be open to what I love about him." We ask her to *breathe* and *move* and even to *play* with that question, *making it bigger, creatively expressing* her questions about the issue. She takes a deep breath before she gets up. As she warms to trying something different, she says, "I must control you! You must do as I command!!" Then she begins to laugh at herself. "I am the Wizard!" Now she wants to go find a wizard hat and really play.

We move to *appreciating*: What does she appreciate about herself, about Frank? Now that she's been playing, this is easy for Joan. "I appreciate that I'm organized. I love that he isn't, that he's a free spirit. I've always admired that about him, how he marches to his own drummer."

Loving what is? That's easy now that Joan feels more expanded. To remind herself what love feels like in her body, Joan closes her eyes and imagines her beloved dog. She breathes into that love, filling her body with it. Then she thinks about her relationship with Frank and surrounds that thought with the same loving vibration. She relaxes and sighs. She has come through the channel into Creative Brain and now can imagine the huge potential that the two of them have together.

It's time to get out the Internal Compass. What does Joan really want? She starts with "I want Frank to be more responsible." Hmm. Is that what she really wants, the bottom line? "No. Let's see. I want to worry less." OK, that's closer, but we're not there yet. "I want to feel free, have my life feel open and full of possibility." Ah. We've landed.

After locating herself, Joan used Shift Tools to change her energy from contraction to expansion, and in doing so, she moved from Reactive Brain to Creative Brain. She started with anger directed toward Frank but was able to sail through the channel into the zone Above the Line. Here she was able to move through Neutrality and Acceptance into Appreciation and Love. While in Creative Brain, she could finally land in the truth about what she really wants.

Now let's walk through this process with Frank. Frank starts out resistant—maybe this is one more way he'll give himself up!—but moves through his resistance into being Willing; now he can begin to traverse the channel. Here's what he describes:

I notice that my whole body feels pulled in. [Noticing] *I feel scared. No, as I tune in to it, actually I'm angry!* [Speaking the Unarguable Truth] *As I hang out with this feeling and let myself feel REALLY angry* [Being Present, using the Bilge Pump], *I can feel it begin to loosen. I wonder what is behind all of this anger?* [Wondering] *I see how I've kept my life small. The truth is that I'm angry about not letting myself be powerful, of always going small, collapsing into being afraid.* [Speaking the Unarguable Truth.] [He stands up straight, pushing his chest out and placing his hands on his hips, and belts out:] *If I were King of the Forest!!* [Moving, Breathing, Playing, Creatively Expressing] *All right, appreciating—I appreciate how many friends I have. And I appreciate Joan for how responsible she is. She always figures out how to pay the bills. I guess I can love all of this, myself for being afraid, Joan for doing the best she can. What do I really want?* [Internal Compass] *Oh, to win the lottery and never think about money again! Well, maybe not. That would be boring. OK, let's see. What do I really want? Hmmm. I want to express my creativity. I want to live a life that is worth living. I want a big life.*

Can you feel the movement from contraction (Below the Line) to increasing expansion (Above the Line)?

Now that both Joan and Frank are out of irons, let's help them reconnect and really get moving again. They take out the Leak Plugger Kit and start to toss ideas and thoughts back and forth until they generate some possible agreements, with the goal of *being allies in helping each other get everything they each want*. Here's how that would sound:

Frank: So you want freedom, and I want a life worth living.

Joan: Yeah, we actually want kind of the same thing.

Frank: I know—weird. I thought you liked it this way!

Joan: Well, I know you haven't been happy.

Frank: No, I haven't.

Joan: Me neither.

Frank: So how do we get freedom and lives worth living?

Joan: Hmm. I guess a budget doesn't really help with that.

Frank: No, I feel tight, tied down. I guess that's why I never did follow a budget.

Joan: I think I've been trying to control you because I feel scared, out of control.

Frank: Really? It's not just that you're a control freak? [Smiling]

Joan: Well, maybe I am. And really? I want freedom.

Frank: How about if we start thinking really big? What if I could help you and you could help me find a way to have freedom and a really big life?

Joan: Oh, that sounds so great! I have some ideas. What do you think?

Frank: I have a million! I've been keeping a notebook of inventions. I've shown some of them to Gary. We've been talking about starting a new business. You know, this reminds me of when we first got together, how we used to dream together.

Joan: You sure are hot when you're dreaming. . .

Does this conversation sound far-fetched to you? It isn't. The shift can happen that fast. Reactive Brain seems to like the familiarity of drama and stuckness; Creative Brain loves expansion, thinking big, dreaming outside the box. With the playful momentum of Creative Brain, the contraction of blame becomes unappealing, so even when there are opportunities for Frank and Joan to lapse back into Reactive Brain, they don't seize them. In Creative Brain, suddenly ideas that were once improbable are now possible. Where there first appeared to be only limited solutions—work harder! Win the lottery!—suddenly the landscape changes as the imagination is ignited. *What if we sold everything and lived on a sailboat? There's freedom and a big life. What if you went back to school to get that degree you've always wanted while I start my dream business?* Joan and Frank have chosen the point on the horizon that they want to aim toward—freedom and a big life—so they can use their Internal Compasses to keep them on course as they co-create what they really wanted all along. And they can use the bottled up energy they were depleting with their stuckness and power struggles to fuel them to go where they really want to go.

Well, maybe that was too easy. Maybe Frank and Joan are exceptions. Now Matt and David, they have real problems, right? This addiction stuff is not going to just shift. Or could it? First, the readings:

- Pressure Gauge

    Both are in contraction. Matt is mobilized; David is immobilized. Their thoughts about the other are generally negative, and they each keep generating contracted responses from the other.

- Inner Map

    Matt is at Pride and Anger. David is at Fear, Despair, Guilt, and Shame.

- Relationship Map

    Matt is stuck at Hero-Villain, with an occasional foray into Victim. David is stuck at Victim, except when he's thinking about Matt—first he goes into Villain with his criticism, and then he becomes a Hero to himself with his justifications about drinking.

- Bilge Pump

    Both are very backed up.

- Leak Plugger Kit

    Both Matt and David are out of integrity in a variety of ways. They aren't making effective agreements; they aren't speaking the unarguable truth; they are stuck in blame and not taking responsibility for how they are creating the issues.

- Shift Tools

    Neither is using any Shift Tools; both are drifting.

- Internal Compass

    Both have lost sight of what they really want out of life; each is simply reacting to moment-to-moment cravings. (Extra points to those of you who have noticed this is very close to what was happening between Joan and Frank. In contradiction to Tolstoy's assertion,[46] all unhappy couples are pretty much alike.)

Let's assume that Matt and David are willing to shift. (It might take some time for this to be true. Meanwhile, the one who is willing can shift without the other one doing anything; this will give the other partner time to be in his own rhythm about shifting.) Matt might start with something like this:

> *I notice I feel nauseated, and my lower back has been chronically in pain. I feel scared, almost panicked. And really angry. Enraged. As I put my attention on these places, let them get even more intense, I'm having a memory of being ten years old. My father got home drunk; there was another big fight, and I got in between my parents. I was so scared! I thought my dad was going to kill my mom, or maybe me. Oh, now I feel really sad. I needed him, and I could never get him to see me. [Taking time to shudder, to cry] I wonder how I've been playing this out with David? The truth is, he's so great, I'm afraid he'll leave me. [Taking time to let the fear move through his body] Yeah, so I've been sabotaging him. If he really gets better, he's more likely to leave me. Well, I guess that might happen. I can't control that. But I want to! [Laughing, gesturing picking at the air, trying to control and manipulate it] And I would be OK. [Getting up, moving around] I want him to stay because he wants to, not because he has to. I appreciate him for how hard he's worked his program. And I appreciate myself for looking at all of this. So now I'm going to just breathe love into all of it, through it all. And I see now that what I really want is for both of us to be happy, to have a whole lot more fun.*

These shifts would typically unfold over time, though the shift could take only a few minutes. The channel from Reactive to Creative Brain is actually quite short; the time it takes to traverse from one to the other depends on the skill of the sailor.

Shall we tune in to David?

> *As I breathe and move, I notice this feeling in my body that I hate. It goes away when I'm drinking. I call it my depression. When I tune in to the sensations, it's this clenching that's always there in my gut and my throat. Yuck. I really want a drink. I can't believe I'm such a wimp! What's the matter with*

me!! OK, right, just the sensations. All right. My throat—it's been this way for years. Maybe I have throat cancer! Umm, yeah, make it bigger—that's sadness. What do I have to feel sad about! That makes no sense. OK, I'm tuning in again. I'm seeing my mom leave. I was five. She eventually came back, but things were never the same. My dad seemed so—gone. I don't know how to explain it. Things were just never the same. [Crying now] *Oh God, I feel like throwing up. Yeah, that's fear all right. See?! I am a crybaby, so weak! That's what my brother said all the time, shut up you crybaby! Mom will leave again if you don't shut up!*

Does David's experience sound extreme? It's not. To be human is to go through losses, events that terrify or enrage us. As children, few of us had support in experiencing our emotions while life was happening around us. We did the best we could to get through, make those feelings go away. David's and Matt's experiences are unique—and they are common. Let's find out what's happening with David now:

All right, so my throat feels more open now, and the nausea is better. [Taking big breaths, shaking out his limbs] *I still like the idea of a drink.* [Laughing] *And I know that has never helped. I've let myself resort to that again. I've been blaming Matt, but I know that's been my choice. I liked being sober. And it was hard. I wonder if I could do it again? I appreciate myself for taking the steps to recovery; maybe I could. One day at a time.* [Taking a step forward on shaky legs] *And I appreciate Matt for believing in me from the beginning. I like just breathing; I'll do that for a sec. What do I really want? I want a full life; I want to spend my time loving myself and loving Matt.*

Now let's put Matt and David together:

Matt: *Wow. I had no idea all that went on for you.*
David: *I know. I didn't get that I remind you so much of your dad.*

Matt: This is some big stuff.
David: Yeah. Oh, well, we're some big guys! [Smiling, taps Matt gently]
Matt: OK, so I guess we both want kind of the same thing.

This exchange is actually so common as to be typical. When couples get down to the bottom line, it is almost always true that they want the same thing, or at the very least, what they each want feels enriching to the other.

David: So how do we get, let's see, both of us being happy, having more fun, and spending our time loving ourselves and each other? Sounds pretty good.
Matt: I know. That's something I can get behind.
David: I'm going back to AA meetings.
Matt: Good idea. I feel scared that you'll meet someone else while you're there. And I can deal with feeling scared.
David: I'll keep you posted about exactly what's going on for me. I haven't been doing that. I can do that.
Matt: I'd love that. I've missed you.
David: I've missed you. [Embracing]

These examples are condensed, and they are based on the real-life experiences of couple after couple who use these tools.

Frank and Joan worked with money issues; Matt and David, with addiction. Let's tackle the next big topic for power struggles: sex. Remember Bonnie and Patricia? First, let's get some readings:

- Pressure Gauge

    Both are in contraction. Patricia moves back and forth between being mobilized and being immobilized as she tries to figure out what to do and then gives up. Bonnie was immobilized, but since she met Danny, is mobilized.

- Inner Map

Patricia was in Anger and Pride; she's now fallen to Shame. Bonnie was in Shame and is now up in Pride and Anger.

- Relationship Map

Patricia started in Hero, spent a lot of time in Villain, and then slid down into Victim (though she becomes Hero to herself when she watches TV and eats cookies and ice cream.) Bonnie has been in Victim for a long time, which was attractive at first to Patricia, and is now to Danny, who has a fantasy of rescuing her from her controlling partner.

- Bilge Pump

You know the answer to that now: the pump is clogged.

- Leak Plugger Kit

While integrity is important to Patricia and Bonnie, they don't want to "hurt each other's feelings," so they leave a lot of things out. Each one has decided that whatever they're thinking is just better left unsaid. They have accepted the lie that life and relationships inevitably lose vitality. They are out of alignment with what they really want, and they aren't taking steps to get back into alignment. Instead, each is letting herself drift along unconsciously.

- Shift Tools

Neither is using any Shift Tools; both are drifting.

- Internal Compass

    Each is drifting in unconsciousness, having lost contact with her real wants.

Now let's talk to Bonnie and Patricia, who have both stepped into their willingness to shift.

Bonnie: I notice my fists are clenching when we talk about this. What is that? Anger?! I don't have anything to be angry at Patricia about—she's been so good to me! [Pausing] *OK, so I get to be angry.* [Standing up, breathing, moving] *Yes, I do feel angry. I think she doesn't respect me. She bugs me about paying her to live here, like I'm a roommate! I thought I was her partner! OOOH, that pisses me off. And she always knows what's right—we could be driving along, she knows we're supposed to turn, or whatever. She has to be the smarter one.* [Moving her shoulders, punching the air] *I've been mad for a long time. When I said I'd move in, I thought this was going to be my house too. But she's never moved her stuff around so I could really move in.*

Feelings that have been building can take time to move through. Let's keep going with Bonnie.

Yeah, I don't even know if I'm in love with her anymore. Sure I love her, but in love—I haven't felt that in a long time. With Danny, I feel good. Like I have something to offer somebody. Not like I'm a nobody. That's what's true. I didn't want to tell that to Patricia, but it's true. [Sitting down, looking visibly more relaxed] *I wonder what's really going on? I guess I lost myself awhile back. I forgot even how to say what I want. I don't even know what I like anymore. Phew!* [Getting up again, spinning slowly around] *Yeah, that's me, just kind of a flake! Ha!* [Shaking her hands out] *No, I can feel me again. I'm here. OK, what I really want is to have a voice again, to have a self. To know where I end and other people start. Ah, yes, I feel my body.*

I like being angry. I appreciate my body. I appreciate Patricia for her great mind. Hmm, yeah, and she does have a verrrry attractive body. . . What I want is for us to get off the damn couch and do something! Get out and dance. I used to love to dance—I still do! And move, and be ALIVE! I want to feel alive and valued, appreciated!

And Patricia?

Well, I feel pretty numb, hearing all of that from Bonnie. And hurt! What did she just say about someone else?! Oh, what? You mean hurt isn't a feeling?? OK. Very knotted up in my stomach. Scared. Terrified!! She could leave! I don't like that! After all I've done for her!! Oh, right, that's blaming. I'm mad. I don't want her to leave. And I'm afraid she will anyway. [Standing up, starting to move around, taking big breaths] She might leave, she might not. [Jumping up and down, making faces] She loves me, she loves me not, she loves me, she loves me not. [Chuckling a little] Well, that's life. I appreciate her so much, though—her mind, she's a smart one, have you noticed? I appreciate myself for being so smart that I picked her! What do I want? I want to create space for both of us to be who we really are. I don't care about being right—it doesn't matter now, does it?

Now let's listen to the two of them:

> *Bonnie: Look, I love sex, too. I know we haven't been having sex.*
> *Patricia: I thought you said you had a low sex drive.*
> *Bonnie: Well, that doesn't seem true right this minute. And I sure felt some great stuff with Danny!*
> *Patricia: Oooh! [Looking angry] I hate that! And—I'm glad you still have those feelings.*
> *Bonnie: I'm not dead. I'm just bored. OK, what I mean is—I haven't been creating much fun with you, in my life.*
> *Patricia: Yeah, I know what you mean. I've been in a definite rut.*

Bonnie: So we both want to feel alive, valued, appreciated, and like there's space for each of us to be who we really are.

Patricia: Yeah, that's a great list.

Bonnie: And I want to add, to have a blast together. To do interesting things.

Patricia: Like taking lessons together or something?

Bonnie: Sure! And how about if we try some new things in the sack? I've got this catalogue . . .

Patricia: Oh, no! [Shocked expression turning to thoughtfulness] Well, OK. Let's look at it later!

The tools you have been learning to use are magical.

Situations that you may have deemed to be completely hopeless (because, of course, your thoughts were generated out of being stuck in Below-the-Line contraction) can spring back to life in a matter of minutes by using your tools and instruments to move through that channel from Reactive to Creative Brain. Just as ships that were wedged on sandbars can be raised by the tide until they gently begin to move again, relationships that seemed hopelessly mired can get unstuck.

The concepts and techniques that you have been learning throughout *The Relationship Ride* have a great deal of power. As you play with these tools, you will get so good at using them that the techniques will become effortless and you will sail with the wind.

The Ultimate Checklist

You can load this checklist of tools and instruments into your duffle bag to use whenever you feel stuck in Hero, Villain, or Victim; when you feel contracted, unhappy, or stressed; if you notice negative or critical thoughts; or if you are stuck in conflict with another (or yourself). This checklist will guide you away from the rocks, help you find the wind to move you out of irons, and get you through any storm.

THE ULTIMATE CHECKLIST

☐ **TAKE YOUR READINGS**

Pressure Gauge: Are you above or below the line?
Inner Map: Locate yourself on your Inner Map. What state are you in: Shame, Guilt, Despair, Sadness, Fear, Anger, Pride? Or perhaps you are in Willingness? How about Neutrality (just being with what is), Acceptance (of the truth of what is), Appreciation, Love, or Joy?
Relationship Map: If you're Below the Line (just taking your readings can shift you), are you in the Villain, Hero, or Victim role?

☐ **GET OUT YOUR BILGE PUMP**

Notice your sensations.
Ride the wave of your emotion.
Express what is true in an unarguable way.
Rest and appreciate yourself.

☐ **USE YOUR LEAK PLUGGER KIT**

What **truth** haven't you spoken?
What or whom are you **blaming**?
What **agreements** haven't you kept?
How have you **gone off course** from your own life?

☐ **USE YOUR SHIFT TOOLS**

Noticing: Notice the sensations that are happening right now.
Being Present: Let yourself be fully present with these sensations.
Say Something Unarguable about those sensations, what emotion you're feeling, what you want, or the stories you're telling yourself?.
Breathing: Take some slow, deep breaths.
Moving: Stand up, move around.
Playing/Making it Bigger/Creatively Expressing: Let yourself do something totally different with your experience. It's OK to play!
Appreciating: What can you appreciate right now?
Loving What Is: Think about someone or something you love; breathe this feeling of love into the issue.

☐ **CHECK YOUR INTERNAL COMPASS**

What is the bottom line of what you **really** want?

You now have at your disposal an extensive list of tools. You don't have to use all of them; one of the pleasures of a full toolbox is having the perfect tool for the job. Increasing your aptitude with any one of them is likely to help you change your course; to be skilled at several will ensure a successful and adventurous voyage.

If you'd like, you can download the Ultimate Checklist from www.JuliaColwell.com.

Exercise 1: Using the Tools in Your Duffle Bag

- Take your readings:
  - Pressure Gauge: Are you Above or Below the Line?
  - Inner Map: Locate yourself on your Inner Map. What state are you in: Shame, Guilt, Despair, Sadness, Fear, Anger, Pride? Or perhaps you are in Willingness? How about Neutrality (just being with what is), Acceptance (of the truth of what is), Appreciation, Love, or Joy?
  - Relationship Map: If you're Below the Line (just taking your readings can shift you), are you in the Villain, Hero, or Victim role?
- Get out your Bilge Pump:
  - **Notice** your sensations.
  - **Ride** the wave of your emotion.
  - **Express** what is true in an unarguable way.
  - **Rest** and appreciate yourself.
- Use your Leak Plugger Kit:
  - What **truth** haven't you spoken?
  - What or whom are you **blaming**?
  - What **agreements** haven't you kept?
  - How have you **gone off-course** from your own life?
- Use your Shift Tools (notice that you've already covered some of them!):
  - **Noticing**: Observe the sensations that are happening right now.

- **Being Present:** Let yourself be fully present with these sensations.
- **Speaking the Unarguable Truth:** Say something unarguable about those sensations, what emotion you're feeling, what you want, or the stories you're telling yourself.
- **Breathing**: Take some slow, deep breaths.
- **Moving**: Stand up; move around.
- **Playing / Making It Bigger / Creatively Expressing:** Let yourself do something totally different with your experience. It's OK to play!
- **Appreciating**: What can you appreciate right now?
- **Loving What Is:** Think about someone or something you love; breathe this feeling of love into the issue.

- Use your Internal Compass: What is the bottom line of what you *really* want?

See Appendix A for a quick reference to the Ultimate Checklist.

Points to Steer By

- Your willingness to be authentic and live in integrity opens you to full participation with whatever life has to offer.
- The chaotic moments that can occur between "something happening" and two (or more) Reactive Brains vying for control are when power struggles are most likely to occur.
- Our reactivity—which leads us to immediately contract into the instinctive safety of a dominance/submission hierarchy—creates the perfect storm of conditions for frustration and stuckness in trying to resolve issues. To take the next step in our evolution, we must forge co-creative partnerships between equals.

- The "romance of rescuing" is a main path into power struggle; few people can maintain the Hero stance over time.
- Being the Hero eventually takes on a parental tone, while being a Victim means becoming childlike.
- The initial compromise of self for security can start a trajectory that leads to long-term problems. The incremental steps toward diminishing ourselves to keep the peace simply cannot continue without leading to a variety of issues.
- Affairs, secrets, drifting, and addictions are often desperate attempts to resurrect a positive sense of self.
- The truth is a tool for ongoing intimate emotional connection.
- The next stage of human evolution in relationships is sharing power. When we are in the Power With territory, we all get to be as big as possible, living our true gifts without threatening anyone else.
- The tools you have been learning to use are magical. Situations that you may have deemed to be completely hopeless can spring back to life in a matter of minutes when you use your tools and instruments to move through that channel from Reactive to Creative Brain.

9

Danger!
Storms and Sea Monsters

*No one would ever have crossed the ocean
if he could have gotten off the ship in a storm.*

~ Charles Kettering

It's time to really challenge your seaworthy skills. You know how to use your instruments, navigate, chart your course, steer, pump out the bilge, plug your leaks; your tools are sharpened and ready to use. You have even been testing yourself on the open sea of relation-ship, getting yourself out of irons and off of sandbars. Now for the ultimate adventure: braving storms and facing the sea monsters that surface in the stirred-up, tumultuous waters.

Are you ready? Many a relation-ship has perished upon the rocks after such encounters. In fact, half of all who set out for the big adventure of *intima-sea* jump ship along the way. Many others stay in the harbor, content to simply dream about the excitement of life far away from all that is familiar. It is unlikely that anything will push you to your limits like a conscious relationship, where you will come face-to-face with your own—and your partner's—most tempestuous internal storms and where unrecognizable monsters will unpredictably attack out of nowhere or slink aboard and try to pull you under.

This chapter is about shining a light into your own darkness. We all have an unconscious part of us, a place where, among other things, we park those aspects of ourselves that we would be dismayed—and sometimes even horrified—to witness. And—returning to the energetic principle of "what we resist, persists"—the irony here is that the more we try to wall off and deny these aspects of ourselves, the more we energize them. As we push down our baser parts, we open ourselves to potentially sparking their energy into unpredictable acting out.

Relationship has its own unique ability to make us behave like threatened animals. Out in the world we might seem civilized, goodhearted, well-intentioned. But put us behind closed doors with an intimate other, and suddenly we are capable of behaviors we don't practice anywhere else. How does this transformation into ugliness happen? How does "such a quiet man" or "a really nice woman" turn into a person whom his or her partner ends up defending against, reacting to, shrinking or flinching or running from, and ultimately hating? It is a strange truth that, though we might view ourselves to be the poor, misunderstood Victim, it is our most intimate others, those to whom we have professed our deepest love, who have sometimes experienced us as the evil, monstrous Villain.

So what are we to do? It is an age-old question, really, one that most religions have organized themselves around: How do we evolve beyond our animal nature? Typical dogma would suggest that we rise above it. Making an effort to split out the "red" energy of lust and rage is popular among those who try to keep the devil out by expressing the more angelic "white" energies, such as prudence, temperance, chastity, and being "nice." While such guidelines for personal conduct have helped move our species out of much of our propensity for brutality and toward becoming more civilized, we have had to pay a price.

Generally, the best we can do is to shut down these impulses, place them where all unacceptable parts of us go: into the unconscious.

Closed off from awareness, those aspects that are most beastly trouble us no more. We might feel shut down, bored, or passionless, but at least we know we are morally superior—that is, until those dark energies are triggered.

It is an unadvertised aspect of intimacy that closeness activates those energies that we have not let ourselves feel or process. The huge connection of initial infatuation creates such an expanded field that those old, contracted emotions that we have been suppressing get drawn up to our awareness. Once we face these feelings and allow ourselves to actually experience them, the dense energy can move and simply dissipate out of our bodies. However, since most of us are not expecting such an uprising of old "stuff" while being close to another, our first impulse is to move away from it by pulling the plug on the connection. It is unnerving to us when our own—or our partner's—untamed self surface. We know we are supposed to be nice and civilized, not animal-like, not beastly, and certainly not monstrous.

When we have nightmares about monsters, the best way to end them once and for all is to turn around and face what is chasing us. Let's do that right now. When you imagine a monster, what comes to mind? It is probably ugly and animal-like, not human. It might be slimy or oozing; it probably has huge pointed teeth and slathering jowls. It could be a fire-breathing dragon with a snapping, powerful tail, or a red-eyed wolf growling and ready to attack. No matter what form our imagined monsters take, they are frightening, unpredictable, out of control, and certainly out to hurt us or to kill us. In other words, our imagined monsters are actually animals—possibly formerly humans—caught in Reactive Brain. And the most frightening monsters of all are those that exist inside of us.

What are the origins of our inner monsters?

It's time to get out your Inner Map and Relationship Map again. Look at the Pride and Anger states Below the Line. Remember that this is also the zone of the Villain and Hero, those who dominate through mobilization to get control. And do you remember that these positions are similar to pack leaders, like alpha dogs or gorillas? Indeed, once we have moved Below the Line into Reactive Brain, we humans share the bestial experience of how animals behave when survival is threatened. From the proud, domineering lion's roar that reminds us of an esteemed politician to the hyena's snarl that calls forth images of greedy corporate leaders, humans who are caught in a fight for dominance look very much like our animal ancestors. And superimposing an animal's primitive impulses on a human is what we mean by "creating a monster."

As we keep moving down the Inner Map to Fear, Sadness, Despair, Guilt, and Shame—those areas of submissive, largely immobilized animals—the parallels between animal and human behavior become stronger. We don't get our typical monstrous images from this part of the Map, but the images of frozen terror in the face of someone encountering monsters are plentiful in our collective consciousness of ghost stories, horror movies, and folk tales.

In other words, when we are in the zone of the Reactive Brain, we inhabit those same states as threatened animals do. Reactive Brain takes us right to the reflexive actions of our animal selves who are facing survival threats: we are ready to strike out, fight, run, or submit in preparation for death. Of course, the evolution of human consciousness has given people access to a vast array of other ways to respond than these; as adults we have many other ways to cope with possible harm. But by the time we reach adulthood, our bodies have stored our multitude of childhood responses, all those times when we had only our instincts to fall back on when dealing with perceived dangers.

As children, every one of us goes through overwhelming emotional experiences at various times of our lives. Whether it is "big T" trauma (like sexual abuse, loss of a parent, or childhood surgeries) or "little t" trauma (such as the first day of kindergarten or being snubbed by peers), growing up is rife with experiences that flood us with more emotion than we can handle. Without support, the only way we can cope with those overwhelming emotions is to divert our attention from them. This is when we first learn not to be emotionally present, as we quickly figure out how to distance ourselves from the too-intense emotional energy that is going on in our bodies. This is basically what "defenses" are: a variety of ways to keep ourselves from feeling what we are feeling.

A main defense children use to protect themselves from having a feeling is to take on the characteristics of those around them. If they feel terrified, they might notice a respected parent's or sibling's rage and learn how to cover their terror with anger. Or maybe they feel sad, but they get the message that it isn't good to cry, so they train themselves to look happy instead. They might disguise anger by the more acceptable emotions of fear, shame, or guilt. This emotional substitution is an unconscious process that happens over time as a child mimics aspects of important people in her environment and as her coping behaviors are reinforced by those same people.

This process of taking on others' characteristics to shield ourselves from overwhelming feelings culminates with the creation of a sub-personality, or persona. A persona is a pseudo-self that comes into being to protect our real, essential self by setting up a wall between the essential self and what it perceives as danger from outside the self. Because personas are born from within Reactive Brain when we sense that our survival is being threatened, their existence is stuck at a state of consciousness somewhere Below the Line. In other words, personas are aspects of ourselves formed from our Reactive Brain to defend our survival. We can leave persona and step into essence when we move through that channel that takes us over the line from Reactive to Creative Brain.

Personas are, by their very nature, parts of us that are stuck at the emotional state they learned from others to protect us from the original overwhelming emotion. Personas are useful; it is their stuckness that causes problems. As you learned in Chapter 2, our thoughts and experiences are determined by our emotional state: everything we perceive is filtered through the state we are in. Remember "attractor energies," how our emotions draw particular responses from others? Since a persona is born from experiences we have when we are Below the Line, that part of us gets stuck at how we perceived the world while we were in that state. And we believe what we learned about the world when we were in that state. In other words, when we're in a persona and are addressing a current situation, we emotionally time-travel to interact with and battle a world that disappeared years before.

> Frank was the third and last son. His parents expected the boys' relationships to be rough and tumble, intervening only when someone started crying. What they didn't notice were the times that playing cowboys and Indians meant that Frank's brothers tied him up and left him, nor did they see that his brothers' teasing was humiliating to Frank. Frank developed several personas out of these experiences: a "tough guy" who knew not to cry because if he cried, the taunting would get worse; a "crybaby" who learned that crying would finally get some help from his parents; and a "viper" who would go into a full-out tear of rage and desperation, punching and biting to try to get his brothers to stop.

> Joan was five when her parents divorced and her dad moved out. Joan adored her father and sat by the front window, futilely watching for him, overcome with sadness and suppressed anger. He finally started coming by and picking Joan up for the weekend, but by then Joan had shut herself off by watching TV and reading. Her mother, dealing with her own life's collapse, drank a lot and turned to Joan for comfort. Joan developed personas to build a wall between her sad self and her situation: a "caretaker" persona who puts aside her own needs to nurture others; a "teaser" who submerges her anger by verbally poking at others; a "numbed out" persona who turns to TV and books to not have to feel; and "the melancholy baby" who gets depressed and believes nothing will ever change.

Over the course of a childhood, we all form many personas. Some of them are functional and help us to be successful in the world. Joan's "caretaker" is an example of a persona that helps her get approval and connection. Personas that exist within the Hero role typically work pretty well for a while. But as we learned earlier, no one can maintain the Hero role indefinitely. It is inevitable to slide into Villain personas (like Joan's "teaser" or Frank's "viper") that lash out to regain a semblance of control. Or to finally give in to Victim personas (Joan's "numbed out"; Frank's "crybaby") when nothing else works, so all that is left is to give in to helplessness.

Thus, every one of us is walking around as a conglomeration of our essential self surrounded by a range of Hero-Villain-Victim personas lying in wait, ready to spring forth should they perceive a situation that has key similarities to the time during which the personas originally formed. They are like a pack of guard dogs circling around our essence, each ready to handle the particular threat it learned is possible in the world.

While this internal structure of personas makes perfect sense from a perspective of survival, it makes us feel crazy. Until we have met and made friends with our personas, we never know when one of them is going to get triggered and take over. There we are, going along, trying to live our lives as reasonable, good people until "something happens" that is reminiscent of an event or a time from our past, and a persona is activated. Without warning, a part of us emerges that we might not like or appreciate, yet it is suddenly steering the boat: the sea monster (or monster in the sheep's clothing of social appropriateness) has taken over.

This instant switch is a perplexing experience for us because we are generally unaware of what triggered us to switch states so precipitously. Meanwhile, this abrupt change can be really disturbing for those around us, who can no longer connect with the person they are used to. It can be so jarring to our intimate other that it is likely to trigger one of his personas, a part that is invested in his survival. With two people in Reactive Brain, the power struggle begins.

Joan and Frank fell in love. Their first months were filled with passionate lovemaking and a sense of being truly seen and known. Joan was attracted to Frank's "tough guy"; Frank enjoyed being nurtured by Joan's "caretaker." Over time, however, Joan felt some anger about always being the one to give up on her needs.

Her "teaser" started to come out, which caused some noticeable bristling in Frank, who began to erect an emotional wall. Joan then tried harder to be nice and sweet, which further evoked Frank's "tough guy"; Joan's "numbed out one" led her to retreat into her books. They started fighting more, with Frank accusing Joan of being mean and Joan telling Frank she was sick of his distance. One night, everything escalated.

Joan pushed for contact by "teasing" Frank; Frank exploded; Joan collapsed into sobs. Frank, feeling himself on the verge of crying, tried to leave; Joan blocked the door. In his desperation, Frank pulled Joan away from the door and threw her against the wall. Joan called the police.

Something else that makes us feel crazy when our personas are activated is that we feel confused, unaware that we are addressing current situations with past emotional responses; we are living in the past and the present simultaneously. We walk around in the world trying to figure out what to do in all kinds of ambiguous situations. When personas step in, they are just applying what they learned a long time ago—with no filters between past experience and present situations. That is what unconscious patterns are—a mechanism for using what we have learned in the past to automatically handle whatever is going on in the present. However, projections really take hold when our triggered perceptions from the past come into contact with present-day reality. Personas are living in the reality they are creating, and it is pretty hard to convince them they are wrong.

During the high romance at the beginning of intimacy, each person gets to experience himself or herself as the most expanded and magnificent of beings. Over time this wonderful sense of self can degrade when we begin to discover—and face—our worst, most dense, and certainly ugliest parts. As one person said to her partner, "You think I'm a monster! Nobody else I know thinks that about me. You bring out the worst in me!" When two people project reality from their sea-monsters selves, they create clashing storms that make them want to jump off the relation-ship. The irony is that these moments of triggering and counter-triggering personas—as we saw with Joan and Frank—hold the potential for the highest degree of personal transformation. Letting the slimy sea monsters surface means that we can finally see what has been under our own surface all along, and so we can begin to tame our own savage beasts.

Taming the Savage Beast

Did you think your seafaring adventure would include encountering masked impersonators? Or that they would be living submerged in you and your beloved? Unlike what we read in the stories of yore, the ultimate set of skills for you to learn is not how to slay dragons or the best methods for luring out and eradicating the serpent scourge. Instead you'll be called upon for something that takes much greater courage: facing all of these inner parts (whether they're civilized or monstrous), accepting them, and even loving them.

Before you learn these most difficult of tasks, let's examine the ineffectiveness of how most people handle these hidden aspects. Here is what does not work very well: trying to make the monsters "nice," disowning them, or letting them run free.

Making Our Monsters "Nice"

Cramming our reactivity into being more civilized is like putting Tarzan into a tuxedo; it works for a while, but the exquisite wildness within is tamped down. Our culture thrives on people channeling their animal power into productivity. However, there is a fine line between being productive and losing one's zest for life by pushing away one's natural impulses. Our society's high rates of depression, anxiety, and addiction attest to that. The "socially rewarded"[47] personas we form are often attempts to make our wild impulses conform to rules so as to not alienate those we love.

Disowning Our Monsters

We have a range of ways to try to disown our monster selves. We refuse to believe we have these dark, ugly aspects, so we see our own monster aspects in others, never recognizing them as our own. This projection results in our desire to punish the person upon whom we project (explaining the huge prison population of the United States). Or we use self-loathing, beating ourselves up in an attempt to control our dark parts, and when we inevitably fail to keep them underground, we turn off our awareness, as if ignoring the monster will make it go away. Our dark parts surface anyway, though we can still resort to just not noticing what we are doing or rationalizing our beastly behavior. Or we use the rigid morality of religion or rules of appropriate behavior to try to push these parts down, hoping they will just go away (the failure of which can be seen in the high rates of incest in the most fundamentalist of religious patriarchs).

Another problem with disowning our darkest aspects is that it requires a fundamental disconnection from ourselves. Many of us make a devil's deal that looks like this: In order to maintain connection with our partner by not displeasing them, we disconnect from ourselves by disowning parts of who we are. When we are disconnected from ourselves, we cannot possibly connect with another. Again, this fundamental disconnection can be observed through the high energetic cost of maintaining our socially rewarded personas.

Even when the disowning method seems to be working, it requires a full shut-off switch, resulting in a complete shutdown of anything that might resemble passionate energy. Initiative, creativity, and sexuality must go. This method explains how partners move from "in love" to "I don't know what happened to what I used to feel—I'm kind of numbed out."

Finally, disowning our personas requires a great deal of psychic energy to maintain. The barriers we create to keep the personas out of our awareness are vulnerable to completely breaking down when we are exhausted or simply sick of trying to be good. The walls will inevitably crumble, and the monsters will come rushing out, free to do whatever they want.

Letting the Monsters Run Free

When all of the squishing-down, splitting-off, and walling-away systems fail and the submerged feelings spring to the surface, no one is better off when our monster selves feel free to express their most base impulses. We can feel an initial release into the freedom of expression, but unfettered, humans are capable of behaving like the most threatened of animals, but with much more developed methods of violence. Without some control over expression, we are willing to belittle, disparage, demean, and humiliate; under more extreme circumstances we are capable of beating, violating, raping, torturing, and killing. Our minds generally come up with good reasons for these behaviors (we couldn't stand it anymore; we were just defending ourselves; there was no choice; we were "following orders"), but what these negative behaviors are truly about is that we let our reactive monsters run the show. As much as we might like to point to others as the evil-doers and try to lock them away, bomb them, or kill them off, the design of our brain makes every one of us capable of atrocities.[48]

The low point of intimate relationships is when our monsters have broken free. This is when arguments escalate into maneuverings for control and dominance. All kinds of unsavory behavior can result when we engage in a fight to be right, from guilt-tripping to put-downs to abusive language and eventually even battering. The brawling partners may go chest-to-chest in an attempt to not lose, or they may resort to the unattractive self-debasing maneuvers of submission: manipulation, childishness, placation, or total collapse. These escalated, monster-persona-driven conflicts are the culmination of the slide from being at our best to showing our very worst selves. Many people cannot stand to stay in a relationship when this eruption of monster-personas happens; other people stay in the relationship by redoubling their efforts to lock the monsters away or by simply filling their lives with addiction and with drifts—those activities that keep them away from their feelings.

It may seem like nothing redeeming can come from allowing our monsters to surface. In fact, here is where staying on the relation-ship can offer rich rewards. Once each person's monsters have emerged, the path to true wholeness is possible. To be whole is to have all parts known and accounted for, where nothing is walled off or pushed away. When we accept our own and our partner's sea monsters, we don't need to hide our personas from ourselves or from each other, which makes our energy available for true co-creativity. Having all hands—even the slimy, creepy, embarrassing, disgusting, brutish ones—on deck means that partners can assemble a team that can dream, create, and fuel passage into territories the couple had never before explored—or even imagined.

Now that you know why serpent slaying won't work, it's time for you to gain proficiencies that are closer to those of snake charmers. Dealing with your own—and your partner's—sea monsters requires first getting up close to them. That's probably the scariest part, to let yourself look into the eye of the beast. Once you have let yourself really get to know those frightening hidden parts, the next step is to actually have a relationship with them. That means talking to them and understanding why they came into being and what their jobs have been all along. The ultimate goal of serpent-charming is to relate to them so well that, when the monsters come to the surface, you can find out what they are trying to tell you while they provide you with fuel to power your ship. If you remember that darkness is just contracted energy—light made dense through compaction—what previously terrified you can become your own nuclear power plant.

Taming the Monster

The first step of monster taming is to let yourself see your own personas. Let's lean over the railing and call them up out of the ocean. Remember that they all exist Below the Line, meaning that the monsters are really just you when you're in one of those Reactive Brain states. The more of them you know about, the better. Some are socially rewarded; others are not.

Let's start with some of the easier personas. These are the ones that you rely on to get you through every day. They work well; other people tend to like them as these personas strive to be socially rewarded. You don't feel particularly expanded while you're in them, but they seem to help oil interactions at work or with other relationships. Here are some examples: Do any of these sound familiar to you?

Socially Rewarded Persona:	Persona Motto:
Pleaser	"How can I help?"
Workaholic	"I'll do it!"
Nice parent	"Why don't you try..."
Nice girl/boy	"Sure! No problem!"
Accommodator	"Whatever you want."
Enlightened one	"It's all good."
Cheerleader	"You can do it!"

Do you get the idea? These are roles that you have developed over time to get approval from others and to be successful at work and in social situations. Now take a few minutes to list some of yours.

On your Relationship Map, look at the states Below the Line to locate the level of each of the Socially Rewarded Personas in the example above. For example, where on the Map is the Pleaser? Yes, up there in Hero territory. The Workaholic is also in the Hero zone, but you can see how easy it would be for a tired Workaholic to start to sag into Villain or even Victim. Finish locating the personas on the list above and then look at your own list. Do you see a trend? Yep—they are all in the Hero zone. Interesting, eh?

Now let's jump in and dive deeper. Let's find the personas that other people don't usually see, except maybe those who are closest to you. You probably don't like these parts of yourself very much and might feel some shame when they emerge. These are the personas that come forward when the socially rewarded ones get tired of being good. These personas carry much of our power, yet we often try hard to lock them away because they can do a whole lot of damage. If the socially rewarded personas are our angels, these are the devils. Remember that whether personas are angels or devils, they are all products of the Reactive Brain, not the Creative Brain. They all use up energy. They all exist in the Drama Triangle.

Here are some examples of personas that are not socially rewarded. Gay and Katie Hendricks call these the Troublesome Personas:

Troublesome Persona:	Persona Motto:
Self-righteous	"No one but me gets it."
Bad guy	"Nothing you do is right."
Meanie	"You suck."
Rager	"$%&**@#!"
Tyrant	"You'd better do what I say!"
Rebel	"Whatever."
Liar	"The truth is…"
Worrier	"What should I do??"
Sloth	"What's on TV?"
Frozen one	"—"
Child	"Help me!"

Puddle	"Woe is me."
Existential despairer	"What's the point?!"

Listing these personas can be a challenge because these are the aspects of ourselves that we spend a lot of time trying not to see. Interestingly, as you make your own list, you will start to see how those parts of you that you might have secretly thought were your "crazy" parts are really just personas. Wonder about how you have judged these when you list a few of your own in your notebook.

This is a good place to stop and take a breath. This deep-sea diving can be difficult as we let old monsters surface. Something to remember through this exploration is that *every one of us* has aspects that exist at every level of the Inner Map. That's what it is to be wholly human. To deny the existence of less attractive personas is to risk projecting these parts onto others while feeling the impulse to act them out *somewhere*, thus requiring a great deal of psychic energy to keep them from emerging. Disowning personas creates all kinds of problems as we project these parts of ourselves out somewhere. Self-righteous positions, rigid religious dogma, and political movements that thrive on dehumanizing the "other" can all come from our unwillingness to connect with our destructive parts. The challenging task of bringing what was in the darkness out into the light can allow you to use your full energy to create, not destroy.

Ready to dive down again?

Now that you have met some of these parts of yourself face-to-face, how about getting to know them better? Wouldn't it be fun to chat with a sea serpent? Creating a relationship with your personas is the best way to influence how they behave. As in any relationship, personas don't react well to being demeaned, yelled at, or cut off. These attempts at controlling them usually result in them taking over when we're not paying attention (which can be disconcerting when we were trying so hard to be "good"). But personas will respond to being seen and heard for what they're really trying to do for us.

Remember that your psyche created every one of your personas at a certain time of your life, generally your childhood, when you had the fewest emotional resources. They arose to protect your essential self and to take care of you in situations that would otherwise have emotionally overwhelmed you.

Personas have always had your best interests at heart. Their methods might be crude, but they emerged through your childhood experiences when you were doing the best you could to figure out life.

It is possible to even have some fun as you get acquainted with your personas. Once you get to know them, you might even find them to be rather endearing. Later in this chapter is a two-stage exercise for you to get to know your personas. The first part is a quick introduction, and then if you would like you can try a more extended dialogue. You can do one or both, depending on how well you would like to know your personas.

Let's start with the Persona Interview developed by Gay and Katie Hendricks.[49] Remember Joan's "Caretaker?" A lot of us have a Hero persona like the Caretaker. To help Joan really get into and then stay in this persona, we'll ask her to fully embody the persona by taking on the posture and gestures of this role. Then we'll keep using the persona name as we ask questions of the persona. She'll answer these questions with the first thoughts that come into her mind so she isn't censoring what the persona is saying.

This process can be quick (though once you get to know some of your personas, you may want to spend more time with them). It is a powerful, effective way for you to have a new understanding of what the persona did for you and to find empathy for it when it emerges from your depths. Remember that your personas are an important part of who you are.

First we ask Joan to take a moment to fully embody the Caretaker by taking on this role's body posture. She stands with one hand on the other, a sweet smile on her face.

Interviewer: So, Caretaker, what's the most important thing to you?

Caretaker: *Making sure everyone is happy and feels good.*

Interviewer: Caretaker, what are you most proud of?

Caretaker: *I'm really good at sensing what will make people happy.*

Interviewer: Caretaker, when did you make your first appearance?

Caretaker: *When I was about five. After my dad left.*

Interviewer: Caretaker, whom did you learn your style from?

Caretaker: *My mother.*

Interviewer: Caretaker, what do you keep Joan from feeling?

Caretaker: *Sad. Scared. Mad.*

Interviewer: Caretaker, what are you most afraid of?

Caretaker: *People being mad at me and leaving.*

Interviewer: Caretaker, what do you most want?

Caretaker: *Connection. To know that people will stay even if they see who I really am.*

Do you get the sense of how the Caretaker came along and protected Joan from her feelings of sadness, fear, and anger when there was no one around to help Joan feel her way completely through the feelings? Now the Caretaker arises when Joan might feel sadness, fear, or anger, giving her a way to distance herself from these emotions. This is an example of how a seemingly positive character attribute is actually a persona existing Below the Line, not above it: While the Caretaker can help Joan feel better, she isn't actually feeling what is true for her. In fact, the bilge accumulates with unfelt emotion when personas block our true emotional experience.

Getting to know these personas is not about trying to make them go away or to tell them they are doing a bad job. It is quite the opposite. Interviewing your personas allows you to begin to establish a relationship with them so that you can influence what they do when they come out. Now that Joan knows something about her Caretaker, she can notice when the Caretaker has taken over; then she can choose to feel the feelings the Caretaker is trying to shield her from. Over time, Joan might be able to simply have these feelings, giving the Caretaker less and less of a job. The rigid Caretaker persona will show up less frequently, allowing Joan's true essence to increasingly shine through.

Note that every persona carries a pearl of our essential self. Joan may, in fact, have a strong nurturing side. Without loosening the grip of the Caretaker, however, it is impossible to know what is truly part of who Joan is at her core.

Here is the second stage to this process: having an extended dialogue with the persona:

> Joan: So, Caretaker, I like who you are, but you've kind of taken over.
> *Caretaker: What do you mean? I do a great job! Everybody likes me!*
> J: Hmm, yeah, you do. But you keep me from having my feelings.
> *C: What's wrong with that??*
> J: I'd like to have all my feelings now.
> *C: I don't think you could handle that.*
> J: I'm ready to try.
> *C: What will I do? I won't have anything to do!*
> J: Yeah, well. Hmm. How about you take over the baking? You could still do that. And take care of the garden.
> *C: I'll think about it.*
> J: Just talk to me. We can work it out.

This sort of conversation establishes a connection between our awareness and what was previously unconscious. And when we're connected with a persona, we can influence its behavior.

Now let's face into a persona that's a little scarier. Let's interview Frank's Viper. First we will ask Frank to embody the Viper in his posture. Frank crouches over and curls his face into a teeth-baring grimace.

> Interviewer: Viper, what's the most important thing to you?

Viper: To protect Frank.

Interviewer: Viper, what are you most proud of?

Viper: I'll fight to the death.

Interviewer: Viper, when did you make your first appearance?

Viper: When I was five. I was sick of getting beat up, so I figured out how to bite and claw.

Interviewer: Viper, whom did you learn your style from?

Viper: My oldest brother. He fought dirty.

Interviewer: Viper, what do you keep Frank from feeling?

Viper: Scared. Happy.

Interviewer: Viper, what are you most afraid of?

Viper: Being killed.

Interviewer: Viper, what do you most want?

Viper: To not have to fight anymore.

Frank hates this part of himself. It is the Viper that reacted and pushed Joan into the wall and that got Frank in trouble with the police. And yet notice how important the Viper has been in protecting Frank. Frank's Viper lives so deep within him that he doesn't surface until the circumstances of Frank's life most resemble those times when the small-boy Frank really felt that his survival was threatened. The Viper learned to strike to protect Frank then, and the Viper comes out when it thinks Frank needs the same protection now.

Now that Frank has started to get to know this persona, he can begin to have compassion for himself as a little boy trying to survive in the jungle of his upbringing with his siblings. This compassion will start a relationship between Frank and the Viper part of him, which means Frank can actually start to befriend the Viper. Now is when the interview can shift into an actual conversation between Frank and the Viper:

F: So, Viper, you've kind of messed up my life.

V: *I know. Whoops. But it had to happen.*

F: It can't happen anymore!

V: *Hmmph. It will if it has to.*

F: Look, you're too mean!

V: *Well, what was I supposed to do?!*

F: I know, I know. You were scared. And you took great care of me. Thanks for that.

V: *Not me! I'm never scared. OK, maybe a little.*

F: It's OK to be scared. It would help for you to tell me you're scared.

V: *Yeah, you're going to call me a crybaby.*

F: No, I won't. Just tell me you're scared, and I'll help you do something that doesn't mess up my life.

If you take a step back from interviewing and dialoguing with these socially rewarded and troublesome personas, you will see what we're up to here. We're using a lot of Shift Tools—Noticing, Being Present, Speaking the Unarguable Truth, Wondering, Breathing, Moving, Playing, Making It Bigger, Creatively Expressing, and even Appreciating. When you use one or more of these actions, you'll move through the channel into your Creative Brain and feel much more spacious and expanded. When you do the opposite—make the persona wrong, shame it, try to wall it off—you create the opposite: more density and contraction. Facing into and accepting these monster parts means letting them have expression while directing that expression into something that can help you.

Exercise 1: Persona Interview

It's time to practice. You can do this exercise out loud or you can write it out in your notebook.

1. Choose one of your personas to interview. Let the persona take over so that when you answer the questions you're speaking in the persona's voice and your body takes on the persona's

posture. Start each question by addressing the persona with its name:

_____, what's the most important thing to you?
_____, what are you most proud of?
_____, when did you make your first appearance?
_____, whom did you learn your style from?
_____, what are you most afraid of?
_____, what do you most want?

2. Now that you're talking to your persona, you may want to continue a dialogue, as we did in the examples of Joan and Frank's persona conversations. Ask the persona any questions you want, but remember to be appreciative, respectful, and curious. See if this persona is willing to have a relationship with you. Write out the dialogue.

Personas as Resources and Energy

Facing into our own darkness, where our menagerie of disowned aspects lives, is one of the most excruciatingly difficult and exposing moves we can make. There is a reason we have an unconscious; it is a great place to cage off whatever we don't like about ourselves. Parading those parts of yourself out where everybody can see them is like the moment someone finally tells you about the spinach in your teeth: you might simultaneously feel grateful and embarrassed that you have been walking around that way not knowing everyone could see it. If, however, you can allow this moment of exposure to occur, you can step into the freedom of knowing a part of yourself that has long been buried. And you have new resources at your disposal, energy that you would previously shut away with the serpent.

You will also find that these aspects of yourself can enrich your relationship. The typical complaint that long-term relationships are boring is exactly correlated with the lock-down of these disowned personas. Befriending these parts of ourselves means being able to divert their reactive energy into authentic responding and creative expression. Setting these personas free, as we relate to them in a new, affectionate way, means our relationships can gain the passion, creativity, and aliveness that was trapped behind the wall we erected to keep them from getting out. We can then see each other for all of who we are, not just our socially rewarded parts. Instead of relationship being about trying hard to be "nice" and to never be "mean," it can become a much more interesting interchange of the liveliness and unpredictability of personas that can finally come out to play.

So what does it look like when we become conscious of and connected with our personas? Let's go back to Joan and Frank's original blow-up, the one that got them into such an escalated place. Here's a summary of what happened:

One night, everything escalated. Joan pushed for contact by "teasing" Frank; Frank exploded; Joan collapsed into sobs. Frank, feeling himself on the verge of crying, tried to leave; Joan blocked the door. In his desperation, Frank pulled Joan away from the door and threw her against the wall. Joan called the police.

When we replay the scene, it might look very different now that they've had time to get to know their personas:

One night, Frank and Joan sat watching TV. Joan got up and brought back some nachos and a beer for Frank. As she placed them on the coffee table, she laughed. "Wow, am I in persona!" she said. "My Caretaker is right here. I think I'm trying to connect with you by giving you food." Frank muted the TV. "Oh yeah, I recognize her. Though I have to say, she's pretty nice to have around! Now that you say that, I'm not really having many feelings myself. I've been in my Tough Guy all day. I guess it started when I got into it with that guy on the phone." "Well, let's get up and move around," Joan suggested (still in her Caretaker persona). Frank groaned. "Oh no, not that conscious crap," (said his Tough Guy). Joan crept out of the room, coming back with a squirt gun. "HeeAAAHHHHH!!!!" she yelled, dowsing him with water, then running out of the room." "Oh no you don't!" he shouted, in hot pursuit, seizing the plant squirt bottle. Suddenly they were both laughing as they chased each other around the house. They fell into a damp heap together, smiling and finding each other, and themselves, again.

Once you add in the cast of characters that are your personas, who knows what play might unfold. The opportunities for creativity are endless because each persona has his or her own way of talking, dressing, and behaving. By accepting and allowing personas to come to the surface, you can change the unconscious dramas that previously unfolded in your relationship and transform them into conscious play-acting that is interesting, fun, and definitely endearing.

Points to Steer By

- The more we try to wall off and deny the darker aspects of ourselves, the more we energize them.
- Closeness activates those energies that we haven't let ourselves feel or process.
- When we're in the zone of the Reactive Brain, we inhabit those same states as threatened animals do.
- This process of taking on others' characteristics to shield ourselves from overwhelming feelings culminates with the creation of a sub-personality, or persona.
- When we're in a persona and are addressing a current situation, we emotionally time-travel to interact with and battle a world that disappeared years before.
- Projections really take hold when our triggered perceptions from the past come into contact with present-day reality.
- The moments of triggering and counter-triggering personas hold the potential for the highest degree of personal transformation.

- To maintain connection with our partner by trying not to displease them, we disconnect from ourselves by disowning parts of who we are. When we're disconnected from ourselves, we can't possible connect with another.
- When we accept our own and our partner's sea-monsters, we don't need to hide our personas from ourselves or from each other, which makes our energy available for true co-creativity.
- The unconscious is a great place to cage off whatever we don't like about ourselves.
- The typical complaint that long-term relationships are boring is exactly correlated with the lock-down of disowned personas. Befriending these parts of ourselves means being able to divert their reactive energy into authentic responding and creative expression.

10

Discovering New Worlds

One doesn't discover new lands without consenting to lose sight of the shore for a very long time.

~ André Gide

What do you think it was like for the first ones—those in a dugout canoe, perhaps—to leave the coastline and head out to sea, believing there must be other places, other people, but having no idea what lay ahead; the first ship's captain to decide there might be a reason to risk death and destruction and sail away, not seeing land for days, weeks, months? What circumstances came together to motivate people to leave all they knew and understood and go off to the vastness of the unknown?

Knowing the human tendency to keep a tight grip on the familiar, when I imagine what it took to get people to go off exploring, I think there must have been a combination of some extraordinary circumstances. Maybe there was desperation, a need for a new source of food or items to trade. Perhaps people were being driven away by warring tribes. Maybe they had to leave for some other reason.

Isn't it just as possible that they wanted to explore, to find out what was "out there"? As they fine-tuned their maritime skills of navigation, creating more detailed maps and better instruments, it seems natural that they would want to see how far their abilities could take them. Humans are naturally curious, and we thrive on the next challenge. Setting out on the open sea must have required a combination of willingness to let go of the known, the wonder of discovering exotic places, and the courage and drive to test one's mettle.

Much of the world is now surveyed, mapped out, known. Certainly there are still distant lands for the most adventurous among us to explore. But if you don't feel like hiking to the top of Mt. Everest or exploring the Amazon jungle, you can still find challenge and risk. There is nothing like the inner world of the self to provide endless new experiences and discoveries. And intimate relationship is unmatched in its capacity for creating opportunities to push us to new heights in encountering our infinitely uncharted selves.

We have entered an unprecedented time in the many millennia of human existence. So much of our collective history has been about scarcity and competition for finite resources. Our drive to feed, clothe, and shelter ourselves has meant that the focus of our lives—and of our politics—has been to compete with each other, acquire and accumulate as much as we can, and be willing to fight to the death in a patriotic fervor that thinly veils our threatened animal nature. In many ways, the stories of humanity are stories of blame, hatred, violence, and war. In that world of "not enough" we naturally have to expend a great deal of our resources protecting ourselves from each other.

With the expansion of the Internet, we now find ourselves in a global community. We can see, converse, and connect with people all over the world with a click of a computer key. The concepts of "us and them," "friend and foe" are losing meaning as it becomes increasingly clear that we need all of us to solve the challenges of climate change, disease, new sources of energy, and world hunger.

This book is about exploring the uncharted territory of relationships—relationships with ourselves, with our intimate other, with family and colleagues. And this book is about moving out of an old paradigm of living in threat, where being in a position of either Power

Over or Power Under are the only options. *The Relationship Ride* is about the voyage of discovery to the brave new world of real power, co-creative power, a world in which *your* ability to live in your full magnificence does not diminish me but instead is an invitation to me to live *my own* biggest life. Increasing the numbers of those who are fulfilled and living out our gifts benefits everyone. Imagine a world in which we support each other in being as powerful as we can be and celebrate our mutual creativity as our fully developed selves add to the vast, swelling ranks of human resources from which we will all thrive.

Humans have had glimpses of this new world, enough to know it is out there. The great sages are like the early explorers, bringing us back news of a radically different way to live. Wise ones in the form of lamas, swamis, monks, nuns, priests, gurus, and renowned teachers of consciousness crisscross the world with their messages of an existence in which all humans can cultivate ever-higher levels of consciousness. Then there follow the pioneers who, upon hearing about this strange but enticing world, have set sail, determined to inhabit that place where it is possible to live lives that could fulfill our highest potential. We can now collect ideas of what this place looks and feels like so that, together, we can try it out, develop it, live it into our daily existence.

Qualities of Living in Real Power

Having made it this far in *The Relationship Ride*, you probably have a good idea of what real power *is not*. It is not being in the Power-Over position, where you might have momentary experiences of control over yourself and your partner but ultimately run into unending power struggles when your partner expresses a similar need for control. It is not being Power Under, where your only methods for getting what you want are indirect—through manipulation, resistance, rebellion, or passive aggressive behaviors. Thwarting your partner might keep you from being bowled over but still won't help you get what you really want. So what does real power look and feel and live like? What is the payoff for using this duffle bag full of tools you've been gathering and hauling around?

You are probably well acquainted with authentic power. You felt that kind of power when you were first getting involved with your partner. It is that blissed-out, exhilarated, totally infatuated state at the beginning, the one people scoff at as temporary or just illusion. It felt so good because that is how it feels to be totally powerful. You were both showing up as your best selves and being seen by the other in your magnificence. It is the feeling of being "met" that many people strive for, the indicator of finding your equal, the one who is choosing to spend his or her time with you because it is so clear how amazing you both are. There really is very little in life that matches the sensation of being one's biggest self—and being seen and valued for it.

There is one experience, however, that feels even better, and that is when our sea monsters—those frightening and shameful aspects of ourselves—appear one by one and neither we, nor our partners, toss them overboard. As they make themselves known and we accept and love them (while gently removing their tentacles from the steering wheel), suddenly there is nothing left to fear about ourselves or our partner. We finally have access to the creative energy that was blocked when we tried to fend off our monsters, and we let ourselves be whole. The feeling we get when we shine light on our mutual dark places can be even better than the feelings we have at the beginning of the relationship, when we probably worked hard to put on our best faces. Now we can see and love each other for our whole selves.

Remember that all of this requires a commitment to adventure. Giving up the false security of "she'll stay with me because she needs me" or "I'll just give up what I want so I don't make him mad" is a first step into choosing the unknown over the familiar. Committing to authenticity takes you right out of the gentle, soothing waters of the harbor of old conditioning and into the realm of the open sea. Deciding to live in integrity allows you to trade in self-numbing predictability for the lively ride of being fully present so you can respond to the moment's call. The return for this trade-off goes beyond just having an exciting life, however; you now can create a relationship that is so interesting and fulfilling that each person will willingly choose it day after day, year after year.

Let's take some time now to savor the qualities of this new world of relationship. Let yourself see this in your mind's eye, feel it throughout your body, really step into this world of endless possibilities and unrealized potential.

What to Expect in This New World

Here is what you can expect in the new world that you and your partner are co-creating:

- Love, appreciation, creativity, and flow. The space of authentic intimacy allows for each person to be seen, known, and loved, as well as to fully express love, appreciation, and our innate gifts and talents. Connection is an energy that is ongoing and unstoppable, no matter what the circumstances.
- When "something happens," each person skillfully uses tools of consciousness to move through whatever comes up and then return to ease and flow. When old patterns of reactivity emerge, we no longer feel as if we've failed; instead, we weather the passing storm and savor the opportunity to develop our abilities to stay conscious and continue to evolve.
- Full authenticity is paramount. Because mutual authenticity is critical in keeping the relationship intact, we cultivate the practice of speaking the truth about how we feel or what we want, and we give this expression plenty of time and space.
- Both people have made a commitment to be fully on board the relation-ship. By being clear about our commitment to the relationship (and to the supporting commitments like

speaking the truth and living in integrity), we pool our energy to fuel the movement of the relationship.

- There is an ongoing spirit of co-creativity and melding of expression of two individuals. When we're in this place of equality and we're confident that it is always possible for both of us to get everything we want, all expressions of the relationship are a combination of aspects of both people, a unique weaving of what each has to offer.
- Couples pool resources with the full knowledge that what is good for one person is good for both. We fully value and embrace the talents each of us brings to the relationship. We contribute money, time, physical energy, creativity, and love, knowing that we are creating a well-functioning team that is more powerful than the sum of its parts.
- We make decisions together playfully, tossing back and forth interesting ideas until each person lands completely in his or her "yes." Instead of landing on what is "right" and holding onto it, we feel the lightness of possibility and the excitement of our willingness to consider the craziest ideas in order to discover the best possibility.
- Letting go of the known allows the future to be much bigger than the past.
- We view life and relationship as opportunities for practicing our skills of consciousness. Knowing that each person is capable of mastering all of the consciousness tools in the duffle bag allows each to have the space to make mistakes without declaring ourselves or the relationship a failure.
- Play and fun are markers of success. This new land isn't a serious place. Laughter, joy, play, and fun are indicators of being in ease and flow together.
- So are big feelings. We celebrate all of the signs of living life as a fully engaged human: expressions of rage, grief, terror—or

irritation, poignancy, trepidation—or ebullient happiness, creative joy, and out-and-out lust.
- We are open to our experiences—individually and as a couple—with an ongoing sense of curiosity and wonder. Questions are more interesting than answers. We live on the edge of the known and are willing to jump into the unknown.
- When power struggles occur, each person can recognize and claim his or her role in creating the stuckness. Taking full responsibility for any result allows for each to easily shift into creating what she or he really wants.
- Energy feels expanded, flowing, and endless. We ride life's cycles in waves, taking time to rest. When energetic leaks or blocks appear, we quickly seal them or clear them away.
- Both people identify fully as the creators of our lives, confident that we are capable of manifesting whatever we dream up together. Co-creating a life together becomes an ongoing wellspring of inspiration, as well as a terrific form of entertainment.
- Committed to being allies, each of us knows we can rely on the other to wake us up when we go unconscious. Since life can be a series of experiences of waking up and then going back into the deep sleep of conditioned patterns, it is invaluable to have a mate who is willing to shake us awake when we've fallen unconscious.
- Over time, each person develops innate gifts and talents so that each day feels meaningful and fulfilling. The relationship supports each person's creative expression. If either of us feels stuck, we know to ask, "How am I not fully expressing myself creatively?"
- As each person increases the capacity to give and receive love, we are also aware when old patterns arise, and we can easily clear them out. Knowing that the expanded energy of love

brings old issues to the surface, we know how to celebrate our ability to move these obstacles to loving out of the way.

What do you think? Is this a world you would like to live in?

Not only is it possible, it is within your reach today, right this minute. You have been learning the tools to create such a relationship world for yourself. Each tool is designed to move you out of the Reactive Brain of old conditioned patterns that your body and psyche created to ensure your survival. If you apply these tools, they will help you move Above the Line into Creative Brain, where you truly can dream the life you want to live and live the life you dream.

Relationship Practices

Here are some other rich practices that will make this new world even more fun to inhabit. They will also help as you venture back out to sea for more great rides. You can try these out anytime and incorporate them into the ongoing life of your relationship.

Giving and Receiving Appreciations

Telling our partner we appreciate them and taking in their expressions of appreciation is one of the most powerful skills available in keeping your relationship on course. John Gottman found that lasting relationships have a 5:1 ratio of appreciations to criticisms; thriving couples have a 20:1 ratio.[50]

Expressing appreciation is like one of those carnival games where you strike the pad with a big mallet—sometimes the indicator goes up just a little; sometimes it hits the bell. Generally, if we appreciate someone for what they do ("Great dinner, Honey!"), the indicator will go up a little. But if we appreciate them for a quality of their character, who they are ("When I look into your eyes, I see the soul of a person who is generous, kind, and a blessing to all of our lives"), we hit the bell.

Take a moment right now to decide whether you want to commit to generating and receiving appreciation. If you do, here are some you can try: What is something you appreciate about yourself? About your partner? Your family? Co-workers? Your life?

Sometimes learning how to appreciate can feel like trying to get a rusty old gearbox to start to work again. Especially if you have been in the blame and criticism habit, expressing appreciation can take the oil of commitment to get things moving once more. As you try it, notice how quickly it will take you up the states of your Inner Map.

Giving and receiving appreciations are magical in their ability to almost instantly create expansion in our sense of who we are. Finally, appreciating your partner and your relationship in front of others can be an especially powerful experience.

Having New Experiences Together

The New York Times reported on a study about "re-inventing date night."[51] The study compares couples who had date nights when they had a familiar experience (like dinner and a movie) with couples who tried out novel, exciting activities. Results showed that couples who tried something different felt a heightened emotional connection and sense of romance. Being together doing new things seems to activate the brain's reward system. So putting the time and creativity into designing new activities can really pay off. Mystery dates, interesting outings, and learning new skills together are examples of what can inject fun and adventure into intimacy.

Co-Creating Ventures

Moving out of drama and power struggle can leave an uncomfortable void. What to do with all of that extra time and energy? Shift your energy to fill your lives with conscious co-creativity, like house projects, interesting vacations, or new businesses. Maybe you will co-write books, poetry, or songs or make music. Raising children and caring for animals are also examples of conscious co-creations. Of course, these are all also opportunities to work through stuckness and power struggles, which could free up even more creative energy.

Sharing Stories about the Relationship

Re-evoking the feelings of in-love-ness can be as easy as recounting the details of what it was like when you first fell in love. For example, if you would like to feel deep relaxation, it helps to go through all of the sensory details of an experience you found relaxing in the past. ("Imagine lying in the sun. Feel the warmth of the sun's rays on your body as you notice your breathing deepen. Let the chair support you as you feel your body getting heavier. Smell the warm summer breeze flowing gently across your cheeks.") Adding this sort of detail when you tell the story of finding each other is a powerful way to bring all of those sensations back to your consciousness.

Maximizing Your Mammalian Selves

Our mammalian brains create challenging circumstances (when we go into fight, flight, or freeze, for example); they also provide many entry points into how to generate times together that feel nourishing and rejuvenating. Certainly, enjoying sexual interactions can take us to very primary and intensely connected places with each other. And there is so much more that can happen. Mammals thrive on skin-to-skin contact; allowing ourselves to lean into, cuddle up, breathe with, and spoon around each other helps soothe our systems. Prolonged eye contact for most humans has a similar effect of settling us down and finding ourselves as we find connection with those who are most important to us. Understanding that mammals have an instant need for bonding when we are sick or cold or when it is dark outside[52] can make us more responsive to our own, and our partner's, instincts. And keeping in mind that most beings' systems get upset during separation can help us build in empathy during these times, as well as coming up with more ways to have ongoing contact.

Dreaming Together

Dreaming into the possibilities of what you want to co-create in the future will help you tap into your most expanded selves.

Writing down intentions or creating vision boards and collages of your goals can give you the scaffolding you need to bring these dreams into reality. Even lying in the grass labeling clouds together can generate the sense of spacious play that couples thrive on. Let yourselves dream as big as you can—then live into your dreams!

It's Time to Set Sail!

You are a well-equipped mariner now. You have the training, knowledge, and tools to steer through the most ferocious storms and to face the sea monsters' probing tentacles as they emerge from the depths of the churning water. When a relationship storm strikes (in the form of escalated conflict) or monsters slither up to the surface (exposing those parts of you or your partner that you wish weren't there), you know the ropes:

- Get out your Ultimate Checklist (see Appendix A or download it from the Duffle Bag at www.JuliaColwell.com). Use all of the maps, instruments, and tools you have.
- Take time to breathe; find your own rhythm in letting yourself remember what you need to remember, shift when you want to shift.
- Don't listen to the sirens of your mind, all of the stories it will tell you ("This will never change!" "I can't stand him/her/me!" "It shouldn't be this hard!")—they'll pull you into the rocks.

Put wax in your ears until you're in safe waters again: Give your mind something else to do, like remembering words to a song or doing a crossword puzzle. When your mind is in Reactive Brain, it does not wish the best for you.

- Tie yourself to the mast. Don't make any big decisions while the stormy seas are casting you about and the serpents are at their most beastly! This is not the time to decide whether you want to be in this relation-ship.
- Love and embrace your personas, but don't let them mutiny and take over the ship. Use your Persona Interview (see Appendix A or download the Persona Interview from www.JuliaColwell.com) to find out who they are; keep conversing with them until you remember that, no matter how scary they might be, they can't hurt you. You are in charge; as you learn to relate to your personas, you'll be able to influence them to do what you want them to do.
- After the storm has passed, get your bearings again. Give yourself time to rest, to breathe, to figure out where you are and find that point on the horizon you were steering toward. Even if you have drifted off course, don't worry; just get out your compass and map and set sail once again!

Fair Winds!

The Relationship Ride is designed to be a well-thumbed manual, a resource to pull out of your bag during a calm spell or when a storm hits or sea monsters attack. When you know that you have the inner resources to find your own way, *The Relationship Ride* can be a companion as you ride the high seas, a place you can return to so you can remember who you really are. You are the explorer, the intrepid sailor going beyond all you have known to find that place of possibility that you know in your heart is there. It is up to you to chart the course to the relationship of your dreams. Keep your eye on the horizon!

So the sea-journey goes on, and who knows where?
Just to be held by the ocean is the best luck we could have. It's
a total waking up!

Why should we grieve that we've been sleeping?
It doesn't matter how long we've been unconscious.

We're groggy, but let the guilt go. Feel the motions of tenderness around you, the buoyancy.

~ Rumi, from the poem "The Buoyancy"

Points to Steer By

- There is nothing like the inner world of the self to provide endless new experiences and discoveries. And intimate relationship is unmatched in its capacity for creating opportunities to push us to new heights in encountering our infinitely uncharted selves.
- We can create a world in which we support each other in being as powerful as we can be.
- Authentic power is experienced during the blissed-out, exhilarated, totally infatuated state at the beginnings of relationships, when both people show up as their best selves and are seen by the other in their magnificence.
- The feeling we get when we shine light on our mutual dark places can be even better than the feelings we have at the beginning of the relationship, when we probably worked hard to put on our best faces. Now we can see and love each other for our whole selves.
- Committing to authenticity takes you right out of the gentle,

soothing waters of the harbor of old conditioning and into the realm of the open sea.

- The space of authentic intimacy allows for each person to be seen, known, and loved, as well as to fully express love, appreciation, and our innate gifts and talents.
- Telling our partner we appreciate them and taking in their expressions of appreciation is one of the most powerful skills available in keeping your relationship on course.
- Our mammalian brains provide many entry points into how to generate times together that feel nourishing and rejuvenating.
- Dreaming into the possibilities of what you want to co-create in the future will help you tap into your most expanded selves.
- Use the tools in *The Relationship Ride* when you need help remembering how to sail back to smooth waters.

Appendix A: Duffle Bag

This appendix provides a quick reference to the tools you've been learning to use. You may want to print the maps and some of the figures for easy reference on your voyage. Here you will find:

- Inner Map
- Emotional States: What they are and how to understand them
- Pressure Gauge
- Relationship Map
- Shift Tools: A quick look to fill your sails
- Internal Compass
- Bilge Pump
- Leak Plugger Kit
- The Ultimate Checklist

INNER MAP

EMOTIONAL STATES

Emotions can be divided into those states we experience while in Reactive Brain (those that use up energy reacting to threat) and the states we experience while in Creative Brain (those that generate energy when there is a shift into creative response). Emotional states can also be placed on a range from most dense (none to little movement, slowest frequency) to most expanded (more to most movement; faster to fastest frequency).[53]

While sequential in order, it is not necessary to pass through one state in order to get to the next one. Being triggered into reactivity means slipping down the emotional chute into whatever state we land in Below the Line; expanding our consciousness means we can start in one lower state and quickly shift into another that is much higher.

These descriptions are about human beings; however, as we begin to understand animals better, it is clear that we share many of these states with our mammalian, and even reptilian, relatives.

BELOW THE LINE

These states are listed from the least energized to the most energized, as you can see on the Inner Map.

IMMOBILIZED STATES

These dense states keep most of our focus turned inward and are often the result of reacting to attacks by people who are important to us. Physiologically, these very low-energy, self-focused states of immobilization keep people "in their place"—that is, in the Power-Under position, which is also the position of the Victim in the Drama Triangle.

- Shame

    When we feel ashamed and humiliated, it is as if our very essence has been threatened. We often respond by continuing the attack internally through self-denigration. When we're ashamed, we feel cut off and shunned from our connection with people who are important to us.

Shame also carries a physiological shutting down and numbing response that animals generate just before being killed. When we experience this frozenness in our bodies, we may translate it into an impulse to kill off ourselves by becoming suicidal.

- Guilt

   The state of Guilt has slightly more energy than Shame but still feels highly contracted. When caught in Guilt, we express hostility and recrimination toward ourselves for our actions, which is slightly more expanded than the feelings associated with Shame, when we attack ourselves for our very existence.

- Despair

   When we feel Despair, our bodies are experiencing a physiologically chaotic response that comes from feeling totally helpless about being disconnected from people (or other beings) to whom we feel emotionally attached. Despair occurs when no one responds to our sobbing and wailing, which are natural protests about feeling disconnected. Despair is the outer expression of our inner experience of abject hopelessness.

- Sadness

   We feel sad when we feel loss—the loss of someone important, the loss of meaning, loss of material possessions, even the loss of our identity. There is some energy in Sadness, particularly when we can actually express our grief. Our experience of heaviness, as well as our tendency to turn our attention inward when we feel sad, can create a respite from our regular life that can give us time and space to adapt to the loss and begin to regenerate our spirit.

- Frozen Fear

    Fear is our response to a threat to our survival. We typically experience two types of fear: frozen (when the threat is so great that our bodies are automatically preparing for death through an anesthesia-like response) and agitated (the classic "flight" response). When we feel frozen fear, it's clear that we're still in the immobilized side of Reactive Brain. However, a great deal of energy is happening in our bodies, expended through hypervigilance and muscle contractions.

MOBILIZED STATES

When in these mobilized states, we are increasingly motivated to place our attention on the external world. Physiologically, these states have increasing amounts of energy as we begin to shift to a Power-Over stance. When we are in the Hero and Villain roles, we typically keep Fear out of our awareness by taking the action of controlling those around us through expressions of Anger and Pride.

- Agitated Fear

    As our energy gets more freed up, Agitated Fear is the classic "flight" response. Our bodies become physiologically mobilized to do something in response to the threat, including getting away from it or trying to control it.

- Anger

    Anger is a natural reaction that occurs when we are *thwarted* or *intruded upon*; energy rises up through our bodies to push through the obstacle or to create a boundary against the intrusion. Anger can hold a great deal of energy so that when we express anger, our words and actions can feel unpredictable and out of our control.

Like gasoline, anger can either be a wonderfully energizing fuel for forward movement or be destructive and explosive.

- Pride

    Pride holds more energy than Anger. However, as it is still Below the Line; when we feel Pride, we're still using up energy, not generating it. We walk tall and feel strong, but our Pride also leaves us open to reacting out of defensiveness. And as "Pride goeth before a fall," it's a short trip from Pride down to Shame.

THE CHANNEL OF WILLINGNESS

Willingness is the gateway, the channel between being Below the Line and Above the Line. *Wanting* to be willing is not the same as *being* willing, which is a palpable sensation of opening to a different way of experiencing reality. Willingness is like the first bit of sunlight that can stream through the clouds of Reactive Brain. Willingness is about actually facing into what is going on within and outside of us, to see and experience what is going on instead of resisting and defending against reality. The only way to get from Reactive Brain to Creative Brain is to traverse the channel of Willingness.

ABOVE THE LINE

These states are listed in the order in which they increase in expansiveness.

- Neutrality

  Once we've crossed the channel of Willingness, the next most expanded state we can shift into is Neutrality. Just "being with" our experience without judging it allows a continued expansion of our consciousness and a beginning sense of generating energy.

- Acceptance

  Accepting what is going on in our inner and outer world allows us to take a big step forward in expanding our consciousness. This acceptance takes us beyond simple neutral noticing as we meet "what is" with our open attention.

- Appreciation

  The emotional state of Appreciation generates huge energy and expanded attractor fields. Meeting our experience with Appreciation opens us not only to viewing reality as beautiful, inspired, and miraculous but also widens our perspective into a whole new world of potential.

- Love

  Accessing the emotional state of Love gives us all a taste of the ecstasy of true divinity. When in this state, we can connect with creative power that we might not have suspected exists in us. The energy of Love is enormously generative and healing.

- Joy

  Joy occurs when we can be in the ongoing energy of unconditional love and kindness to all of life, otherwise known as compassion. When we are in Joy, the beauty and perfection of the world is constantly available to our perception.

Above the Line is where we find enlightenment. It is the territory of sages, avatars, and our most venerated spiritual beings—and it is available to anyone who is willing to go there.

PRESSURE GAUGE

Use your Inner Map and your Pressure Gauge together to take your emotional readings.

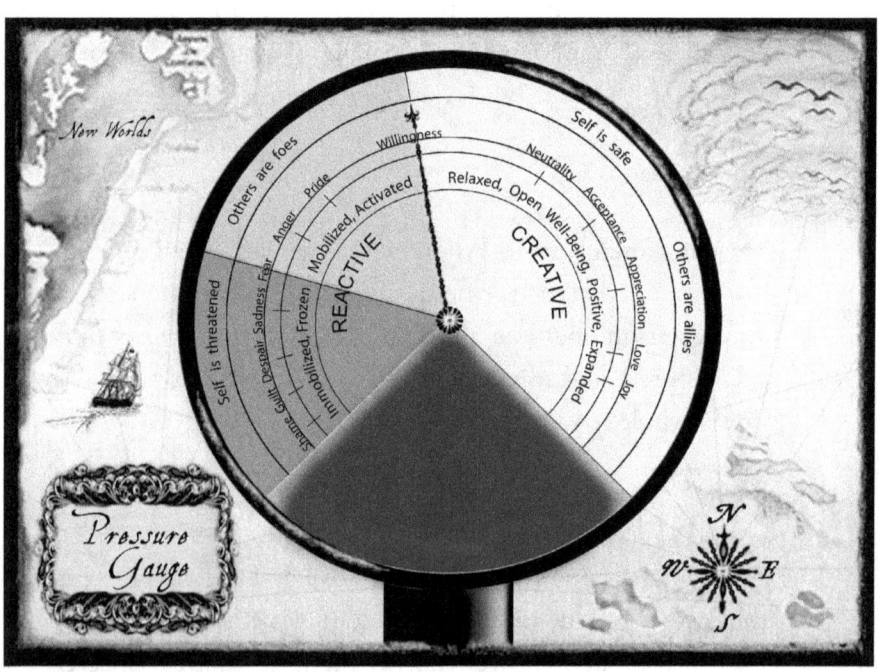

RELATIONSHIP MAP

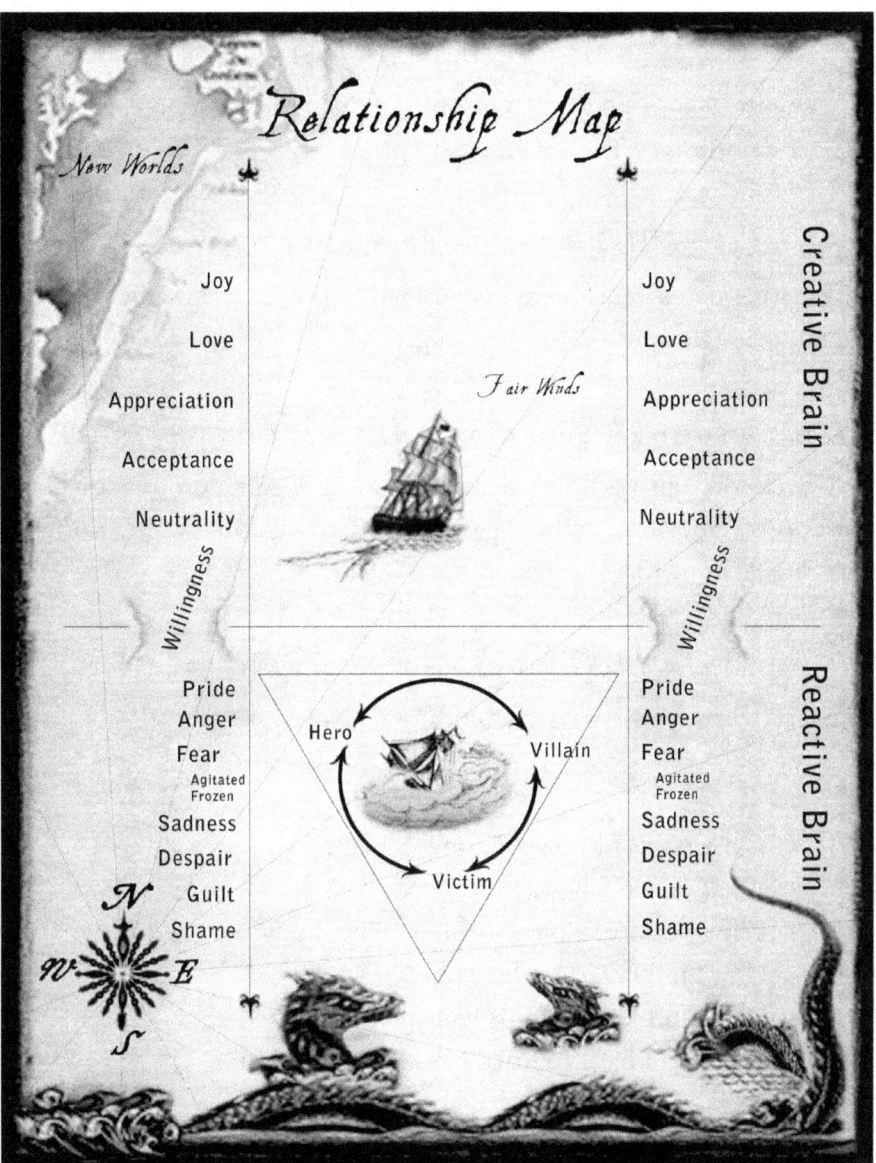

SHIFT TOOLS

SHIFT TOOL #1: NOTICING

Tune in to your body's sensations and read the sensations as signals to your emotions. What are you feeling?

SHIFT TOOL #2: BEING PRESENT

Breathe, pay attention to your breathing, notice thoughts, and return to paying attention to breathing.

SHIFT TOOL #3: SPEAKING THE UNARGUABLE TRUTH

Check for your truth by identifying what is going on in your body: sensations, emotions, knowing what you want/don't want, noticing your thoughts or images.

SHIFT TOOL #4: WONDERING

Start with a satisfying "Hmmmmm." Now ask yourself some big questions:

- What don't I know about who I am?
- What do I really want?
- What does real space feel like in my body?
- How am I creating this issue?
- How am I keeping this issue going?
- What do I have to learn from this situation?

SHIFT TOOL #5: BREATHING

When you notice that you are in Reactive Brain, place your hands on your belly and breathe deeply and slowly, watching as your hands move with the rhythm. Do this for at least a minute. How has your thinking changed?

SHIFT TOOL #6: MOVING

Sit down and make your body still; now move different parts of your body—twirling your finger, clenching and unclenching muscles, wrinkling and unwrinkling your brow. Do you notice a change in your sense of well-being?

SHIFT TOOL #7: PLAYING

Sit still until you have an impulse. When you have the impulse, follow it. Then wait for the next impulse—and the next—until you are simply creating a chain of following the next surge of energy that your body produces.

SHIFT TOOL #8: MAKING IT BIGGER

Whatever is happening for you, exaggerate it. If you notice yourself resisting to shifting, let yourself complain in a loud, whiny voice about how THIS IS REALLY, REALLY HARD!

SHIFT TOOL #9: EXPRESSING CREATIVELY

Write in your journal, create a poem, tell a story, play music, or paint, draw, dance, or sculpt your experience. Or use a different voice tone to sing your experience or express it in a made-up language or sculpt it in air.

SHIFT TOOL #10: APPRECIATING

Look around and ask yourself what you appreciate. If your answer is "nothing," try harder.

SHIFT TOOL #11: SPEAKING WHAT YOU REALLY WANT

Use your Inner Map and your Internal Compass to find your full-body Yes and full-body No. Speak what you want from this place.

BONUS SHIFT TOOL: LOVING WHAT IS

Think of someone or something you love easily and let the feelings of love get so big that they fill your whole chest, then your torso, then your whole body. Marinate in these sensations of love. Now think about your life and turn your loving attention on *what is* and watch your experience of it expand.

INTERNAL COMPASS

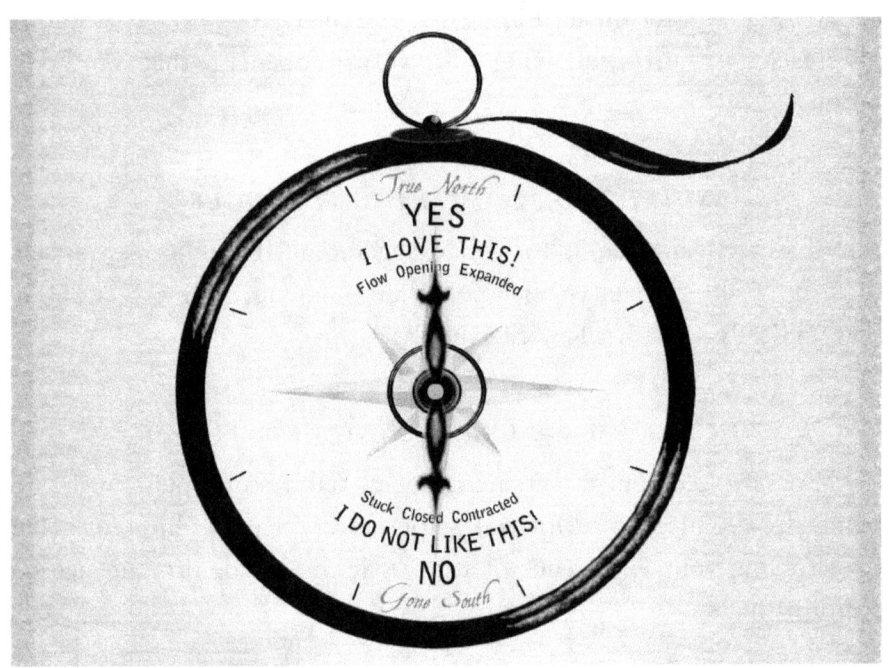

BILGE PUMP

1. Locate yourself on the Inner Map.
    - Are you Above the Line or Below the Line?
    - If you're Below the Line, is there a current threat to your survival? If so, do something! RUN! FIGHT! FREEZE! If not, continue this process.

- Notice that your body is in Reactive Brain, even though there is no current danger to you.
- Don't believe anything you're thinking.
- Celebrate this opportunity to move out old, unprocessed emotion.

2. Notice your sensations.
    - Where are they in your body?
    - What do your sensations feel like? (Tight, knotted, fluttery, queasy, or something else?)
    - Are you feeling mad, sad, or scared?
    - Are these sensations familiar from childhood?
    - How old do you feel?
    - What does this remind you of?

3. Ride the waves!
    - Breathe into the sensations, letting them get as big as they are.
    - Keep your attention on the sensations themselves, bringing your attention back when your mind wants to divert you with thoughts.
    - Keep going through the waves' peaking, until the sensations dissipate.

4. Express what is true.
    - Match the sensations with any expression you want: making sounds, moving, drawing, writing about what is unarguable, even sculpting in the air.
    - Now that you know what is really going on, is there someone you'd like to tell about your experience?

5. Rest.
    - Appreciate your courage for heading straight into your own storm.
    - Notice what your body feels like without that layer of old energy stuck in it. Feel the flow that has always existed beneath the density of that bilge.

LEAK PLUGGER KIT

TRANSPARENCY

- Leak—Not telling the truth (including lies of omission).
- Plug—Practice impeccable transparency: Make this commitment to yourself and to your partner right now: *I commit to speaking the truth.*

100% RESPONSIBILITY

- Leak—Blaming or not taking 100% responsibility.
- Plug—Step into your full creativity: Shift into 100% responsibility by asking these questions:
  - How am I creating this?
  - How am I keeping this going?
  - What am I getting out of things being this way?

AGREEMENTS

- Leak—Making agreements that don't work.
- Plug—Make powerful agreements: Practice making effective agreements in which you and your partner:
  - Agree to what you each will do. Make only those agreements you want to make (guided by your Internal Compass).
  - Feel good about what you've agreed to. Don't make agreements you don't want to make (using your Internal Compass without fail).
  - Follow through easily on the agreement. Renegotiate the agreements you want to change or agreements you no longer want to have.

COMPLETION

- Leak—Letting tasks or agreements remain incomplete.
- Plug—Commit to completing tasks or agreements: Fill out the Incompletion Inventory in Appendix B.

ALIGNMENT

Leak—Being our of alignment in your life.
Plug—Live your true life. Answer this question (as many times as it takes): Am I willing to live the life I really want?

THE ULTIMATE CHECKLIST

☐ TAKE YOUR READINGS

Pressure Gauge: Are you above or below the line?
Inner Map: Locate yourself on your Inner Map. What state are you in: Shame, Guilt, Despair, Sadness, Fear, Anger, Pride? Or perhaps you are in Willingness? How about Neutrality (just being with what is), Acceptance (of the truth of what is), Appreciation, Love, or Joy?
Relationship Map: If you're Below the Line (just taking your readings can shift you), are you in the Villain, Hero, or Victim role?

☐ GET OUT YOUR BILGE PUMP

Notice your sensations.
Ride the wave of your emotion.
Express what is true in an unarguable way.
Rest and appreciate yourself.

☐ USE YOUR LEAK PLUGGER KIT

What **truth** haven't you spoken?
What or whom are you **blaming?**
What **agreements** haven't you kept?
How have you **gone off course** from your own life?

☐ USE YOUR SHIFT TOOLS

Noticing: Notice the sensations that are happening right now.
Being Present: Let yourself be fully present with these sensations.
Say Something Unagruable about those sensations, what emotion you're feeling, what you want, or the stories you're telling yourself?.
Breathing: Take some slow, deep breaths.
Moving: Stand up, move around.
Playing/Making it Bigger/Creatively Expressing: Let yourself do something totally different with your experience. It's OK to play!
Appreciating: What can you appreciate right now?
Loving What Is: Think about someone or something you love; breathe this feeling of love into the issue.

☐ CHECK YOUR INTERNAL COMPASS

What is the bottom line of what you **really** want?

Appendix B: Ship's Locker

This appendix contains a few extra toys and whats-its to add to your duffle bag:

- Persona Tables
- Persona Interview
- Incompletion Inventory
- Core Self Analysis

PERSONA TABLES

Socially Rewarded Persona:	Persona Motto:
Pleaser	"How can I help?"
Workaholic	"I'll do it!"
Nice parent	"Why don't you try…"
Nice girl/boy	"Sure! No problem!"
Accommodator	"Whatever you want."
Enlightened one	"It's all good."
Cheerleader	"You can do it!"

TROUBLESOME PERSONA: PERSONA MOTTO:

Troublesome Persona:	Persona Motto:
Self-righteous	"No one but me gets it."
Bad guy	"Nothing you do is right."
Meanie	"You suck."
Rager	"$%&**@#!"
Tyrant	"You'd better do what I say!"
Rebel	"Whatever."
Liar	"The truth is…"
Worrier	"What should I do??"
Sloth	"What's on TV?"
Frozen one	"—"
Child	"Help me!"
Puddle	"Woe is me."
Existential despairer	"What's the point?!"

PERSONA INTERVIEW

Choose one of your personas to interview. Let the persona take over so that you're speaking in the persona's voice and your body takes on the persona's posture. Start each question by addressing the persona with its name:

_____, what's the most important thing to you?

_____, what are you most proud of?

_____, when did you make your first appearance?

_____, whom did you learn your style from?

_____, what are you most afraid of?

_____, what do you most want?

This Persona Interview was created by Gay and Katie Hendricks and is used here with their permission.

INCOMPLETION INVENTORY

In each of these areas, determine what actions you will take and when.

Money

- How much you owe or others owe you
- Actions you avoid taking to create more security in your life
- Being fully aware of how money is flowing in or out
- Being in alignment with one's true calling

Relationships

- What needs to be spoken and to whom
- Emotions you're having that you haven't yet faced

Physical World

- Car
- Home
- Body
- Physical clutter

Creativity

- Creative projects
- Letting yourself be creative

Expression

- Words you haven't spoken
- Experiences from the past to be faced
- Emotions you haven't processed

CORE SELF ANALYSIS

Part 1: Discovering Your Life Purpose

1. If someone came in right now and aimed a gun at you, demanding to know what your life purpose is, what would you tell them?
2. In the next five minutes, write down everything you can think of that you've always enjoyed or loved to do. Don't think too much—just write.
3. Now consider this: What are those things you love to do that you lose yourself in? That you can't wait to do? That you'd choose to do over anything else? That you had fun doing?
4. Circle the top five items on your list, the ones that take you closest to True North on your Internal Compass. Let yourself marinate in the idea of spending the majority of your time doing those things.
5. Imagine that you're lying on your deathbed looking back over your life. Did you accomplish what you wanted to? What was that?
6. OK, it's time to get your ship in the water. Finish this sentence: To be fulfilled, I will live out my life purpose, which is to . . .

Here are some examples of actual life purposes people have imagined:

- I invite dreams.
- My purpose is to love everyone and everything.

- I'm here to help humans create a new and loving relationship with animals.
- (My own): I'm a friendly elevator operator, joining people as they move up and down the ladder of consciousness.

Part 2: Creating Effective Intentions

Verbalize your intentions in the positive: "My intention is that I live in abundance" instead of "My intention is to not be poor," and write it in the present tense. To help you out, here are six areas that will get you started on listing your intentions.

Who you are in the world:

- Example: My intention is that I live in love and appreciation every moment.
- Now you: My intention is . . .

Relationships:

- Example: My intention is that I continually expand into love with my partner. Yours: My intention is . . .

Health:

- Example: My intention is that I create perfect health, making choices every day that support my well-being.
- Yours: My intention is . . .

Inner World/Spirituality:

- Example: My intention is that I take time every day to cultivate my relationship with my inner self.
- Yours: My intention is . . .

Career:

- Example: My intention is that I create a meaningful and fulfilling career path.
- Yours: My intention is . . .

Money:

- Example: I live in an ongoing flow of abundance.
- Yours: I live . . .
- Keep your intentions list handy and speak them out loud every day.

Notes

INTRODUCTION: SHIP OF DREAMS

1. Gay Hendricks and Katie Hendricks, *Conscious Loving: The Journey to Co-Commitment*, New York: Bantam, 1990.

2. Thanks to Neale Donald Walsch for the idea behind this image. Neale Donald Walsch, *Conversations with God: An Uncommon Dialogue, Book 1*, New York: Putnam, 1995.

3. John Gottman, *Couples Therapy: A Research-Based Approach*, Clinician Video Series, 1997, Gottman Institute.

4. Thomas Lewis, Fari Amini, and Richard Lannon, *A General Theory of Love*, New York: Vintage Books, 2001.

5. John Gottman and Nan Silver, *The Seven Principles for Making Marriage Work*, New York: Three Rivers Press, 1999.

6. John Gottman, *Why Marriages Succeed or Fail: And How You Can Make Yours Last*, New York: Simon and Schuster, 1994.

CHAPTER 2: GETTING YOUR BEARINGS: THE INNER MAP

7. Thanks to David Hawkins for his brilliant taxonomy of emotional states according to their level of energy, upon which the Inner Map is based. David R. Hawkins, *Power vs. Force: The Hidden Determinants of Human Behavior*, Carlsbad, CA: Hay House, 1995.

8. Hawkins, *Power vs. Force*.

9. Ibid.

10. Ibid.

11. Lewis, Amini, and Lannon, *General Theory of Love*.

CHAPTER 3: GETTING YOUR BEARINGS: THE RELATIONSHIP MAP

12. Lewis, Amini, and Lannon, *General Theory of Love*.

13. Ibid.

14. Ibid.

15. Steven Karpman, "Fairy tales and script drama analysis," *Transactional Analysis Bulletin*, 7 (26), (1968), 39-43.

16. Lewis, Amini, and Lannon, *General Theory of Love*.

CHAPTER 4: STEERING TO CATCH THE WIND

17. Les Fehmi and Jim Robbins, *The Open-Focus Brain: Harnessing the Power of Attention to Heal Mind and Body*, Boston: Shambhala/Trumpeter, 2007.

18. Eckhart Tolle, *The Power of Now: A Guide to Spiritual Enlightenment*, Novato, CA: New World Library, 1999.

19. Temple Grandin, *Animals in Translation: Using the Mysteries of Autism to Decode Animal Behavior*, New York: Scribner, 2005.

20. Doc Childre and Howard Martin, *The HeartMath Solution: The Institute of HeartMath's Revolutionary Program for Engaging the Power of the Heart's Intelligence*, New York: Harper Collins, 1999.

21. Thanks to Katie Hendricks for this playful and accurate language.

22. Tolle, *Power of Now*.

23. Kathy Juline, "Awakening to Your Life's Purpose," *Science of Mind Magazine*, October 2006.

24. Todd Kashdan, *Curious?: Discover the Missing Ingredient to a Fulfilling Life*, New York: Harper Collins, 2009.

25. Mary Desmond Pinkowich, "Medicinal Mirth: The Health Benefits of Laughter," *Ode Magazine*, August 2009.

26. Grandin, *Animals in Translation*.

27. Katie Hendricks, personal communication.

28. Childre and Martin, *HeartMath Solution*.

29. Esther and Jerry Hicks, *Ask and It Is Given: Learning to Manifest Your Desires*, Carlsbad, CA: Hay House, 2004.

30. Katie Hendricks, personal communication.

31. Gay Hendricks, *Learning to Love Yourself: A Guide to Becoming Centered*, New York: Simon and Schuster, 1993.

CHAPTER 6: DRAIN THE BILGE

32. Thanks to Katie Hendricks for her terrific notion of "tossing."

33. Ibid.

34. Daniel Goleman, *Destructive Emotions: How Can We Overcome Them?: A Scientific Dialogue with the Dalai Lama*, New York: Bantam Dell, 2003.

CHAPTER 7: RUNNING A TIGHT SHIP

35. Hendricks and Hendricks, *Conscious Loving.*

36. Special thanks to Gay and Katie Hendricks for these questions. Answering them when I was in the middle of a power struggle was my first experience of the power of their work.

37. Gay and Katie Hendricks, personal communication.

CHAPTER 8: RUNNING AGROUND — MOVING AGAIN

38. Gay Hendricks and Katie Hendricks, *The Four Pillars of Integrity* (unpublished).

39. Caroline Myss, *The Three Levels of Power and How to Use Them,* audio recording, Boulder, CO: Sounds True, 1994.

40. Original Karpman Drama Triangle terms were Rescuer, Persecutor, and Victim. Karpman, "Fairy tales and script drama analysis."

41. The term "power over" was first coined by Mary Parker Follett, a turn-of-the-twentieth-century educator and social theorist. Mary Parker Follett, *Prophet of Management: Celebration of Writings from the 1920s,* ed. Pauline Graham, Frederick, MD: Beard Books, 2003.

42. Rosalind Barnett and Caryl Rivers, *Same Difference: How Gender Myths Are Hurting Our Relationships, Our Children, and Our Jobs,* New York: Basic Books, 2004.

43. Lewis, Amini, and Lannon, *General Theory of Love.*

44. Barnett and Rivers, *Same Difference.*

45. Hendricks and Hendricks, *Conscious Loving.*

46. The original first line of Leo Tolstoy's *Anna Karenina* is "Happy families are all alike; every unhappy family is unhappy in its own way."

CHAPTER 9: DANGER! STORMS AND SEA MONSTERS

47. Thanks to Gay and Katie Hendricks for this term.

48. Philip Zimbardo, *The Lucifer Effect: Understanding How Good People Turn Evil*, New York: Random House, 2007.

49. The Persona Interview was developed by Gay and Katie Hendricks. I use it here with their permission.

CHAPTER 10: DISCOVERING NEW WORLDS

50. Gottman, *Why Marriages Succeed or Fail*.

51. Tara Parker-Pope, "Reinventing Date Night for Long-Married Couples," *The New York Times*, February 12, 2008.

52. Lewis, Amini, and Lannon, *General Theory of Love*.

53. These descriptions are inspired by David Hawkins' Map of Consciousness.

www.ingramcontent.com/pod-product-compliance
Lightning Source LLC
Chambersburg PA
CBHW051352290426
44108CB00015B/1980